COMMENDATIONS FO

CW00920323

"What does the blessed life look like d
gullible disciples misdirect many int
life marked by buoyant health, bubb
— as if Jesus died to give us more ca
But the writers of this blessed book on the blessed life rightly tell us otherwise. Anchored clearly in Scripture and deeply rooted in Christ, this book reminds us that the blessed life is a far richer, deeper and better way of living because it is rooted in Christ and guided by his word and Spirit to a life of faith and obedience to God. The blessed life brings glory to God and leads to true and lasting human flourishing that carries within it a great weight of glory in the present and for the future far much greater than the ephemeral life-destroying popular message of "blessing" many of us hear today. I highly recommend this book to everyone especially to my African brothers and sisters so that together we will live a truly blessed life in Christ for his fame and our joy."

**Bishop Felix Clarence Orji, Diocesan Bishop of the
Anglican Diocese of the West and Coordinating Bishop of the
Church of Nigeria North American Mission (CONNAM)**

"This is a beautiful book. These words of Jesus and the apostle Paul will bless you as they are opened up. Give this to a new Christian for them to be established in good and godly living; give this to someone older who needs to return to their "first love". Read and you will want to read again."

**Bishop Keith Sinclair, National Director of the Church of England
Evangelical Council (from April 2021)**

"As a Latin American Anglican this book has been a tremendous blessing for my brothers and sisters in Chile and South America. It has given us a better understanding of good biblical and Anglican theology. I really thank Dr Lee Gatiss for giving us a book like this. We needed an initiative like this very much!"

Bishop Enrique J. Lago, Anglican Diocese of the South of Chile

"I like the approach of this book. On each topic the reader first encounters a substantial scripture portion leading to a pertinent startup question which is then followed by a particular Bible text from which is drawn a devotional application. This is rounded off each time with some reflective questions and a concluding prayer. I also enjoyed the book's overall development which begins with Jesus talking about the blessed life followed by a deepening application of this to our lives and to our sins. This compact book has assembled 32 authors from around the world including several from Africa, whose writing is warm-hearted, direct, and confrontational. Yes, we are made to face our sinful tendencies and the ugly fruit our sins can bear, but each brief section always supplies hope by pointing us back to Christ. Part of the book's engaging development is the climax in the final chapters on Christ's death on the cross. *The Blessed Life* shows that our blessedness is ultimately rooted in what the Son of God accomplished for us on the cross."

Revd Dr Mark Dickson, Principal of George Whitefield College, Cape Town, South Africa

"*The Blessed Life* is an immensely helpful production from the Church Society. With a wonderful diversity of contributors from around the Anglican world, this short book reflects upon an array of Scriptural sentences and subjects in an accessible way for all sorts of people. In a time when Global Anglicans need to drink deeply from the well of the Word, this publication offers good spiritual refreshment in the gospel of the Lord Jesus Christ."

Revd Dr Mark Earngey, Lecturer at Moore Theological College, Sydney and Editor of the *Australian Church Record*

the
BLESSED
LIFE

**Reflections on the Beatitudes,
the Fruit of the Spirit,
the Seven Deadly Sins,
and Jesus's Words from the Cross**

Edited by Lee Gatiss

The Blessed Life: Reflections On The Beatitudes, The Fruit Of The Spirit, The Seven Deadly Sins and Jesus's Words From The Cross
Edited by Lee Gatiss

The views expressed by the authors of individual chapters in this book do not necessarily represent those of Church Society.

© Church Society/Lost Coin Books, 2021.

Published for Church Society by Lost Coin Books, London.
email: lostcoinbooks@gmail.com   LOST C●IN
web: www.lostcoinbooks.com

Church
Society
EQUIPPING GOD'S
PEOPLE TO LIVE
GOD'S WORD

Church Society
www.churchsociety.org
admin@churchsociety.org

Church Society, Ground Floor, Centre Block
Hille Business Estate, 132 St Albans Road
Watford WD24 4AE, UK
Tel +44 (0)1923 255410

ISBN 978-1-9993270-9-5

Contents

INTRODUCTION

In this book, we will be reflecting on some of Jesus's first words, as well as his last, and pondering what the Bible says about the spiritual life. That is, we will be reflecting on the Beatitudes from Matthew 5, Jesus's words from the cross in the Gospels, the fruit of the Spirit from Galatians 5, and the so-called seven deadly sins which the Bible speaks about in various different places. At the start, Jesus tells us how to live a blessed life. At the end, we see how his own blessed life concluded. In between, we learn how to be blessed ourselves as we die to sin and live for him, filled by his Spirit.

In the opening of his Sermon on the Mount, Jesus tells us nine times what a blessed life looks like. 'Blessed are the poor in spirit,' he says, 'for theirs is the kingdom of heaven. Blessed are those who mourn, for they will be comforted.' These surprising and arresting pronouncements undercut worldly expectations—'Blessed are you when people insult you'! They also teach us to live in a way that pleases God, always looking to the future where he will put everything right.

In Galatians 5, the apostle Paul contrasts the acts of the flesh and the ninefold fruit of the Spirit. The way of true freedom in Christ is about living in a way that keeps in step with the Spirit of God who has been sent into the hearts of his children. The world, the flesh, and the devil urge us to live for self, but the Spirit produces in us something which changes our orientation in life and bursts out of us with love, joy, peace, forbearance, kindness, goodness, faithfulness, gentleness, and self-control. These things are a blessing to us, and to others around us.

Paul speaks about the acts of the flesh which oppose the Spirit as 'sexual immorality, impurity and debauchery; idolatry and witchcraft; hatred, discord, jealousy, fits of rage, selfish ambition, dissensions, factions and envy; drunkenness, orgies, and the like.' He warns us that 'those who live like this will not inherit the kingdom of God.' The Bible also mentions other such eternally deadly sins, and over time the traditional (but not exhaustive) list of these became pride, greed, lust, envy, gluttony, wrath, and sloth. Protestants don't need to follow medieval teaching on the differences between venial and mortal sins and so on in order to benefit from reflecting on these seven sins, which we are to crucify with all their passions and desires.

As he hung on the cross for us, dying to take the punishment which our sins deserve, the Lord Jesus is reported to have spoken seven times. The famous last words of the God-man, who lived the most truly blessed life that anyone ever lived, help us better understand what our priorities should be. Christ exemplified the blessed life of the Beatitudes; full of love, joy, faithfulness, gentleness, and self-control, he offered himself unblemished by deadly sins through the eternal Spirit to God. So we will reflect on his eloquent words from the cross, as we approach Easter, looking for his resurrection and the joy that was set before him.

I hope you will enjoy and be edified by these reflections. We've managed to assemble a great cast of contributors, Anglicans from five continents (including writers from Australia, New Zealand, South Africa, Tanzania, Nigeria, the United States, Chile, and the UK), men and women who minister as archbishops, bishops, parish clergy, theological educators, college or prison chaplains, or in various other ministries as gifted lay people. I pray that you will be blessed by all they have written, as we think together in these chapters about what a truly blessed life looks like.

Lee Gatiss
Director of Church Society
Cambridge, UK

the BEATITUDES

1. The Poor in Spirit

Bible Reading

Matthew 5:1-12

Now when Jesus saw the crowds, he went up on a mountainside and sat down. His disciples came to him, and he began to teach them. He said:
'Blessed are the poor in spirit,
for theirs is the kingdom of heaven.
Blessed are those who mourn,
for they will be comforted.
Blessed are the meek, for they will inherit the earth.
Blessed are those who hunger and thirst for righteousness,
for they will be filled.
Blessed are the merciful, for they will be shown mercy.
Blessed are the pure in heart,
for they will see God.
Blessed are the peacemakers,
for they will be called children of God.
Blessed are those who are persecuted because of righteousness, for theirs is the kingdom of heaven.
'Blessed are you when people insult you, persecute you and falsely say all kinds of evil against you because of me. Rejoice and be glad, because great is your reward in heaven, for in the same way they persecuted the prophets who were before you.

Starter Question

At the start of Jesus's longest recorded public teaching, what themes are you surprised to see or not see?

Today's Text

Now when Jesus saw the crowds, he went up on a mountainside
and sat down. His disciples came to him, and he began to teach
them. He said:
'Blessed are the poor in spirit,
for theirs is the kingdom of heaven.'
Matthew 5:1-3

B efore we focus in on our specific verses, there are a few
things to note about verses 3-12, which are known as the
Beatitudes. These beautiful attitudes focus on the kingdom of heaven, verses 3 and 10 serving as bookends, and promise
blessing in every single verse. They have a structure, flowing from
and into each other, and they are addressed to both disciples and
crowd, so two types of hearer are in view.

Turning to the first few verses, our text for today, we consider
three questions about poverty of spirit: What is it? Why is it a
blessing? And how might we gain or grow in it?

Poverty of Spirit

At school I was never very good at the high jump. I'm sure it
was fun for my classmates to watch, but I was a total failure. I
couldn't clear a bar of even medium height. The great news as Jesus
starts his preaching about the Kingdom of God is that there's no
high bar to clear, but rather a call to lowliness—an invitation to
humility, a normality-inverting charge to pursue being "poor in
spirit"—because in Jesus's revolutionary kingdom, the way up is
always down.

As Jesus teaches his followers, and the crowd listen on, he ex-
plains that kingdom blessings are not for the self-satisfied, self-
sufficient, or proud. Instead, entry to the kingdom is by coming to
the end of ourselves and our own capacities, what has been called
'a healthy sense of self-despair'. Imagine the encouragement this

was to an early follower who knew they understood little, could never live a life good enough for God, and was looking to Jesus for everything. And imagine the challenge to an observant Pharisee trusting in his own righteousness.

THE BLESSING OF SPIRITUAL POVERTY

Why is being 'poor in spirit' a blessing? The simple answer is that 'theirs is the kingdom of heaven.' Being poor in spirit is the necessary qualification to be saved and in the Father's eternal kingdom. To become a follower of Jesus, all you need is need. Tragically some members of the crowd then, and hearers of the gospel today, fail to enter the kingdom because they're not needy enough: their self-sufficiency keeps them out.

The second answer is to understand this saying as a doorway to the other Beatitudes, and indeed the whole Sermon on the Mount (Matthew 5-7). To have come to the end of your tether will motivate and enable you to mourn sin (verse 4), be meekly teachable (verse 5) and keenly seek godliness (verse 6), which will include the attitudes and lifestyle associated with mercy (verse 7), purity (verse 8), peace-making (verse 9) and distinctiveness (verses 10-12).

A third answer is to ask what sort of people you'd most like in your office, family, or friendship groups. The attitudes which we've seen flow from being "poor in spirit" are a great blessing to all whom they impact. Jesus showed that perfectly, and his followers will too, in increasing measure.

GROWING IN SPIRITUAL POVERTY

How can we grow in being 'poor in spirit'? Simply by the gospel: what do we bring to God's great work of salvation? Only the sin which requires Christ's death on our behalf. As David sang: 'Who may ascend the mountain of the LORD? Who may stand in his holy place?' (Psalm 24:3).

As we read on through these stunning and challenging verses, and even on into the following chapters, we will find ourselves fleeing back again and again to verse 3, to re-enter Jesus's doorway to blessing. Our humble, dependent striving to live out Jesus's challenging portrayal of the kingdom cannot be solved by works (which lead to '*pride* of spirit') but by allowing the gospel to humble us more fully. Verse 3 always and naturally leads on to those which follow, so we shall come back there again and again.

Indeed, reading on into the Sermon on the Mount, many of Jesus's lines seem designed to lovingly lead us back there. In God's sight a nasty word is murder and a lustful look adultery (5:22, 27), and understanding this leads to poverty of spirit. Reviewing our giving, praying, and fasting (6:1-18) and considering whether our living is focused on either eternity or now (6:19-34) will develop that poverty of spirit. Any reflection on specks and planks and judgmentalism (7:1-5) will do the same. And thus throughout Jesus's great sermon we are having poverty of spirit developed in us.

Not a high bar in sight—what a relief! I could never jump high enough. Rather, here is the Christ-like glory of lowliness and poverty of spirit, the gateway to great blessing.

QUESTIONS FOR REFLECTION

1. What signs of being 'poor in spirit' can I see in myself and thank God for?
2. How might growing increasingly 'poor in spirit' bless me, and then others through me?
3. What do these verses teach me to pray for myself, for my Christian brothers and sisters, and for the lost?

Prayer

Almighty God, who alone can humble the proud
and delights to exalt the humble:
remove from our hearts the sin of pride,
and replace it with poverty of spirit,
that we may enjoy the blessings of your kingdom in
increasing measure, thinking and living more and more
like your King, our Saviour Jesus Christ,
in whose humility we glory,
and through whom alone we are saved,
Amen.

Andrew Towner *is Vicar of Houghton and Kingmoor in Carlisle Diocese, and Chairman of Church Society Council.*

2. Comforted Mourners

Bible Reading

Isaiah 40:1-2
Comfort, comfort my people,
    says your God.
Speak tenderly to Jerusalem,
    and proclaim to her
      that her hard service has been completed,
        that her sin has been paid for,
      that she has received from the Lord's hand
      double for all her sins.

Starter Question
What is the comfort of the gospel?

Today's Text
Blessed are those who mourn,
for they will be comforted. *Matthew 5:4*

In the word of God, the Bible, we read passages about mourning or weeping, grief and sorrow. For example, the only son of the widow of Nain had died. She and those with her were weeping. Jesus comforted her and, of course, Jesus raised him from the dead soon after (Luke 7:11-17). Similarly, in John 11, we read about the death of Lazarus. When Jesus arrived at the home of Mary and Martha in Bethany, he found them in deep grief because of the death of their brother. Jesus himself wept, although a short while later he called Lazarus out of the grave. In Africa, no doubt as is the case in other parts of the world, people do mourn and they mourn for a variety of reasons: death, illness, persecution, and other forms of loss. We could say mourning is an everyday reality. But in our passage today, the Lord says, 'Blessed are those who mourn, for they will be comforted' (Matthew 5:4).

Those who mourn
Generally, 'those who mourn' refers to people who have feelings of sorrow, distress, grief, or suffering. I can identify three levels or sources of mourning:

- **Mourning because of situations of pressure and pain,** such as torment, oppressions, suppression, desertions, and afflictions from different sources as well as sympathising with other people who are in such situations.
- **Mourning because of situations of need,** such as illness, hunger, homelessness, loss of loved ones, or loss of possessions. As these socio-economic needs are experienced, there will certainly be mourning.
- **Mourning because of the realities of sin.** In this case, those who mourn are conscious of their sins. They may be conscious of sin as a matter of their nature, as they struggle with temp-

tations and the desires of the flesh. They are conscious of the consequences of sin; of the unbelief in their hearts; of their sinning against a God of love and grace; of grieving the Holy Spirit, and of dishonouring Christ. They are also conscious of the sins of others and of the profaneness and wickedness that abound in the world. Because of these and other realities of sin, they mourn.

It is possible to suggest that those who mourn for any reason will be comforted. But the immediate literary context of Matthew 5:4 (namely, verses 3 and 5), suggests that it is those who mourn because of, or in relation to, sin who will be comforted. Clearly, the Lord's primary thought was about mourning because of the realised 'poverty of spirit' just spoken about in verse 3. Mourning in this verse therefore refers to that entire feeling which the sense of spiritual poverty brings about. It refers to grieving due to sin and its realities.

Thus, there is mourning which is a mere natural effect of passion; there is worldly sorrow which works unto death; and there is godly sorrow which 'brings repentance that leads to salvation and leaves no regret' (2 Corinthians 7:10).

THEY WILL BE COMFORTED

Christ declares that those who mourn will be comforted. The promise implies the special comfort that the mourner needs, that is, the sense of pardon and peace and of restored purity and freedom. It is important to note that in the time that Christ gave the Sermon on the Mount, there was a general yearning expectation that prevailed among the hearers for comfort (e.g. Simeon was waiting for the comfort or consolation of Israel, in Luke 2:25). Thus, those who have committed sin and are afflicted and wounded by it, and feel that they have offended God, but are grieved by sin in the world and long for God's grace and mercy, shall find comfort in the gospel.

Comfort in this context entails a sense of the forgiveness of sins, peace with God, clear discoveries of his favour, and the sure hope of our heavenly inheritance. Even so, all present comfort is partial, interrupted, and short-lived. Ultimately, the days of mourning shall end and then God shall wipe away all tears from the eyes of those who mourn (Revelation 21:4). Then, in the fullest sense, shall those who mourn be comforted.

The promise to be comforted is only for those who mourn because of, or in relation to, the realities of sin—and choose to repent and accept the provisions of the gospel. The declaration of 'blessedness' applies not to everyone, but only to those who mourn in that sense.

Questions for Reflection

1. What does 'mourn' refer to in Matthew 5:4?
2. How does God comfort those who mourn?
3. Does God comfort people who do not profess Christ as Lord and Saviour? Why or why not?

Prayer

Almighty God,
thank you for the privilege of meditating
on the teaching of your Son, our Lord Jesus Christ.
By your Holy Spirit, bring those who are yet to believe
the gospel
to the realisation of their sinful state,
and their need for a Saviour.
Grant that we may all understand,
that in our mourning, grief, and godly sorrow
you are the God of all comfort.
Our God, we thank you and pray in the name of our
Lord Jesus Christ, Amen.

Emmanuel Mbennah *is a former biblical studies professor and University Vice Chancellor and now the Tanzanian Ambassador to Harare, Zimbabwe. He is the author of* The Mature Church *(Wipf & Stock, 2013).*

3. Meek Heirs

Bible Reading

Psalm 37:7-11

Be still before the Lord and wait patiently for him;
do not fret when people succeed in their ways,
    when they carry out their wicked schemes.
Refrain from anger and turn from wrath;
    do not fret—it leads only to evil.
For those who are evil will be destroyed,
    but those who hope in the Lord will inherit the land.
A little while, and the wicked will be no more;
    though you look for them, they will not be found.
But the meek will inherit the land
    and enjoy peace and prosperity.

Starter Question

When you see someone getting away with wrongdoing, or building their success on sin, how does that make you feel? How do you respond when you are the injured party?

Today's Text
Blessed are the meek, for they will inherit the earth.
Matthew 5:5

According to David in Psalm 37, the likely responses to other people acting wrongly or unfairly are anger and 'fretting', that is, futile worrying and frustration. That's certainly how I feel in those situations. I'm angry that other people are getting away with things they shouldn't, and I'm even angrier if I am the one who has been hurt by their actions. I'm frustrated when there doesn't seem to be a way to stop it, or to give them a taste of their own medicine. I'm worried that they'll go on and do more and worse.

In place of this frustration, worry, and anger, and instead of retaliation or revenge, Psalm 37 tells us to be still before the Lord and to wait patiently for him. If we give in to our natural responses, David says, that will lead us into sin. What we're told to do is hope in the Lord, and wait for him. Because it is the meek who will inherit the land.

Jesus confirms this in the Sermon on the Mount, saying 'Blessed are the meek, for they will inherit the earth.'

What is meekness?
The Greek word for meekness in Matthew 5:5 is quite often translated 'gentleness' in the New Testament. Gentleness does indeed capture one important aspect of this quality: meekness is not violent or aggressive; it is not arrogant or self-serving. But meekness is not identical to gentleness. As Psalm 37 indicates, meekness specifically concerns our responses to wickedness and injustice.

To understand what meekness entails, we have only to look at Christ himself. Jesus did not retaliate when they hurled insults at him, he made no threats when he suffered, and instead he entrusted himself to him who judges justly (1 Peter 2:23). When Jesus instructs us to turn the other cheek towards those who have already hurt us, or to hand over more to those who have already taken advantage of us (Matthew 5:39-40), he is teaching us what it will mean to follow his own example of meekness in the face of unjust suffering.

This is not the same as pretending that wickedness doesn't matter or that injustice didn't happen. It's not okay for people to mistreat us. It's not. But with meekness, we can recognise that it is okay for us to bear those hurts now while we leave it to God, praying and trusting that he will set them right one day. Meekness doesn't promise an immediate reward, but there is a promise for the future: 'the meek will inherit the earth.' Sometimes God hears our prayers and sets things right here and now, but even when he does not, we know that one day, all the wrongs will be righted, all the injustices set straight, and those who have borne them faithfully, patiently, meekly, will receive their inheritance.

Meekness does not deny that we have rights, but it does mean that we will not always insist on our rights. It means that in some situations we may choose to waive our right to fair treatment, or our right to be free from harassment or bullying. It means that we will not seek retaliation or revenge, though if we can act to prevent others from being hurt in future, we should certainly do so. And although we may feel righteous anger at the sinful actions which have harmed us, we take care that this does not tip over into vengeful anger, by bringing it to the Lord.

Meekness and suffering

So, is Jesus telling us that Christians must be doormats? Is he saying that we must turn the other cheek in an abusive situation? Are we really to give up fighting for justice and righteousness in this world? By no means! Jesus was no doormat and certainly no friend to injustice or wickedness. There are three important things to remember here:

First, while we may choose to waive our own rights, we are not free to waive anyone else's. You may choose to swallow an insult or let an injustice go on your own behalf but you cannot compel that choice for anyone else. Indeed, as God's people we should be actively seeking justice for the weak and vulnerable, and advocating righteousness in all situations.

Second, we are not to seek suffering for its own sake. There is nothing godly about provoking people to lash out against us, and there is nothing to be gained by suffering for our own wrongdoing (1 Peter 2:19-20). Meekness should not be mistaken for the lie of low self-esteem that we deserve to be mistreated.

Third, we are free to remove ourselves from situations where we are being harmed. No one should be compelled to remain in an abusive relationship. No one has to continue working in a place where they are bullied. If you are living in a country where Christians are persecuted, and you are able to leave, then there is no Christian requirement to stay. You may choose to do so, but you are free not to.

THE PROMISE OF MEEKNESS

Meekness does not come naturally to any of us. It is a fruit of the Spirit (Galatians 5:23) and the product of wisdom (James 3:13). It is only because we have been forgiven that we are able to forgive. It is because Christ has suffered for us that we can bear our own suffering. Meekness is an embodiment of the gospel of grace: we will not inherit the earth by fighting for our rights, demanding justice or seeking vengeance. Rather, by meekly enduring through this life, we will receive our glorious, gracious, eternal inheritance.

Blessed are the meek, for they shall inherit the earth.

Questions for Reflection

1. How does Jesus demonstrate this kind of meekness throughout his earthly life?
2. In what sorts of situations are you most tempted to retaliate or to stand on your rights? What would it mean for you to respond meekly instead?
3. How does the eternal perspective of Matthew 5:5 help us to be meek in the present day?

Prayer

Merciful Father,
who sent your precious Son
to patiently suffer injury and bear injustice
for our sake:
grant that we may follow his example of meekness.
Give us grace to swallow insults and set aside
our rights.
Teach us never to retaliate nor seek revenge.
Instead, may our eyes be set on our eternal inheritance
and our hearts trust in your everlasting justice,
through Jesus Christ our Lord. *Amen.*

Ros Clarke *is the Associate Director of Church Society and Course Leader of the Priscilla Programme.*

4. Righteous Appetites

Bible Reading

Romans 7:14-19, 24-25a

We know that the law is spiritual; but I am unspiritual, sold as a slave to sin. I do not understand what I do. For what I want to do I do not do, but what I hate I do. And if I do what I do not want to do, I agree that the law is good. As it is, it is no longer I myself who do it, but it is sin living in me. For I know that good itself does not dwell in me, that is, in my sinful nature. For I have the desire to do what is good, but I cannot carry it out. For I do not do the good I want to do, but the evil I do not want to do—this I keep on doing... What a wretched man I am! Who will rescue me from this body that is subject to death? Thanks be to God, who delivers me through Jesus Christ our Lord!

Starter Question
What is your worst habit?
Why do you do it and why can't you stop?

Today's Text

Blessed are those who hunger and thirst for
righteousness, for they will be filled. *Matthew 5:6*

We know two things about the self-help industry. The first is that it's very profitable. Every January, the bookshops are stacked high with countless titles offering you a slimmer body, great productivity, or a happier life. The tone mostly flatters and assures you that you're special, you're worth it, and you deserve to be a better you. And that you can be.

The second thing we know is that self-help books don't really work. If they did, we could help ourselves and stop buying self-help books. We would only need to buy one and everything would be fixed. We'd be better people and continue to improve.

People who go on diets tend to try lots of diets, because the evidence suggests that most of them don't work in the long term. Business-types who want to be more productive buy multiple books because not one single book helps them to be as productive as they'd hoped to be. Some say you should answer all emails immediately. Others that you should only answer email for 20 minutes a day at 5.00am after you've been for a run.

The problem is this: We like the idea of 'the new you'. But no matter where you go, what you do, or what book you read, you are still the old you. It would be wonderful to say that new life in Christ makes you healthy, wealthy, and wise, but that is never promised in this life to the measure that we might like.

Spiritual striving

Spirit-filled Christians (not that there's any other kind) hunger and thirst for righteousness. Jesus says that to strive and strain for godliness and holiness is a blessed thing. It is the struggle. Our media, both mainstream and social, love to rage against the machine, and blame the system. To them, the problem is bad politics, deceitful or corrupt science, or hateful philosophies. But we know that the main problems in the world are greed, pride, and lust which rage in all our hearts and minds.

In Romans 7, we see how our two natures are at war in the life of the apostle Paul. Read those words again, and don't get too hung up on what he means by law. Read it more like a poem, a Psalm of David. Paul cries out that he knows what he should do. He wants to do it. But he can't! And the very thing that he does, is the very thing that he hates. *Gah!* The pain and regret leap off the page. It's the kind of rage we might scream when running around the house looking for keys (like I do every other day). The inevitability and rage is coupled with despair that we seem to be in an inescapable loop.

If the apostle Paul, who was able to cheerfully withstand persecution and chains for the sake of the gospel, feels this kind of disappointment with his own godliness, we shouldn't be surprised when we experience this too.

Not only is Paul frustrated by his sins of commission, but also by his sins of omission. In verse 18, he expresses his desire to do what is good, but is full of regret that he cannot do that thing. Verse 24 is a fitting climax to this struggle: What a wretched man I am! Who will rescue me from this body that is subject to death?

FREEDOM FROM DESPAIR

Many of us feel that struggle. We feel powerless to control our sinful nature. We go to bed feeling we've done so few of the things we set out to do that day. The things we wanted to avoid we've lapsed into. Again. But Paul's question in verse 24 is not rhetorical, as it would be in a secular book. Nor is it a cry of despair. Who will rescue me?

The answer to our frustration is not to lower our goals, or decrease expectations. It is to praise God. Our own spiritual performance is not the most important thing in the world. We are delivered from our self-loathing, impatience, and pride by the death of Jesus Christ on the cross: Thanks be to God, who delivers me through Jesus Christ our Lord!

We need to make peace with this life-long struggle, hungering and thirsting for righteousness. We need to think less of ourselves, and more of Christ who has saved us from the penalty for sin, and its ultimate power, but not its alluring presence. Not yet. That is in the world to come, where we will be filled with the things we hunger for.

In the Beatitudes, Jesus is reassuring us that our current frustrations and disappointment will end. We will be filled. In fact, we are filled with the Holy Spirit, who gives us the power to accept and engage in the battle, even though it continues until Christ returns in glory.

QUESTIONS FOR REFLECTION

1. What do you do that really bothers you and why does it bother you? What effect does that have on the people around you?
2. What sin is behind that frustration?
3. Have you repented of that sin? Have you asked for God's help with that sin? Reflect on how Jesus has already saved you from that sin.

PRAYER

Lord God in Heaven,
who did not spare his Son, for the sake of our sin,
who sent him to the cross, to take away our iniquities,
who raised him up to the heavenly realms where he
now reigns in glory, and who sent his Holy Spirit to
dwell in our hearts:
grant us, we pray, humility in our struggles to live
aright, a desire to repent for our transgressions,
and the grace to receive forgiveness time after time,
until Christ returns, when pain, regret, fear and
frustration will be no more,
and we will see the true majesty of our Lord and
Saviour Jesus Christ, in whose name we pray. *Amen.*

James Cary is a comedy writer for the BBC, author, podcaster, and a lay member of General Synod for the Church of England as well as the Archbishops' Council.

5. Merciful Mercy

Bible Reading

Matthew 18:21–35

Then Peter came to Jesus and asked, 'Lord, how many times shall I forgive my brother or sister who sins against me? Up to seven times?' Jesus answered, 'I tell you, not seven times, but seventy-seven times. Therefore, the kingdom of heaven is like a king who wanted to settle accounts with his servants. As he began the settlement, a man who owed him ten thousand bags of gold was brought to him. Since he was not able to pay, the master ordered that he and his wife and his children and all that he had be sold to repay the debt. At this the servant fell on his knees before him. "Be patient with me," he begged, "and I will pay back everything." The servant's master took pity on him, cancelled the debt and let him go. But when that servant went out, he found one of his fellow servants who owed him a hundred silver coins. He grabbed him and began to choke him. "Pay back what you owe me!" he demanded. His fellow servant fell to his knees and begged him, "Be patient with me, and I will pay it back." But he refused. Instead, he went off and had the man thrown into prison until he could pay the debt. When the other servants saw what had happened, they were outraged and went and told their master everything that had happened. Then the master called the servant in. "You wicked servant," he said, "I cancelled all that debt of yours because you begged me to. Shouldn't you have had mercy on your fellow servant just as I had on you?" In anger his master handed him over to the jailers to be tortured, until he should pay back all he owed. This is how my heavenly Father will treat each of you unless you forgive your brother or sister from your heart.'

Starter Question
What motivates you to live a distinctively Christian life of self-giving?

Today's Text
Blessed are the merciful, for they will be shown mercy.
Matthew 5:7

According to its website, Pay It Forward Day is marked in over 80 countries. It puts into practice, for one day, the notion in Catherine Ryan Hyde's novel *Pay It Forward* (and the movie adaption by the same name), that one person doing a good deed for another person leads the recipient to do good for someone else, thereby creating a ripple effect and cycle of good deeds. In theory, the giver is to expect nothing in return, but, interestingly, all the reasons listed on the 'Why Pay It Forward' webpage are about the upsides for the giver not the recipient. It seems that even Pay It Forward Day is about the self.

The question of motivation—why we do something—is messy, especially when it comes to doing good. Not only are we complex, finite, sinful human beings, in relationships with people like ourselves (complex, finite, and sinful), but our hearts are deceitful (Jeremiah 17:9).

Jesus's fifth 'beatitude' is about mercy. In fact, it is the only beatitude where the two parts of the verse match each other: the merciful will receive mercy.

Showing mercy
Mercy in Matthew's Gospel is associated with forgiveness and compassion. Sinners need mercy (Matthew 9:13; 18:33). Those who seek healing from Jesus cry out for mercy (9:27; 15:22; 17:15; 20:30–31). Mercy graciously meets need—whether cancelling a debt of sin or relieving the misery of suffering—and showing mercy is contrasted with rule-keeping religious observance (9:13; 12:7; 23:23; Hosea 6:6). On any reckoning, mercy is beautiful, both to give and to receive.

But why are we to show mercy? Taken in isolation, this beatitude might seem to say that before we can be blessed or receive mercy from God, we must start the cycle of mercy ourselves. A case of paying it forward so we can find ourselves on the receiving end. But, of course, such a view would be mistaken. God owes a debt to no person (Job 41:11; Romans 11:35). Whatever this beatitude is saying, it isn't that mercy begins with us!

The first three beatitudes have already told us that God blesses or approves of those who know they are running on empty, who know they are spiritually bankrupt, who grieve over sin and its effects, and who know the humility that comes from honest self-appraisal.

The fourth beatitude then tells us the only realistic response to this spiritual poverty, which is to have a deep longing for God to fill us with the righteousness that is a defining mark of his kingdom (5:10, 20). The mercy, purity of heart, and peacemaking of the next three beatitudes are the outflowing of this gift of righteousness in our lives.

THE BEGINNING OF MERCY
In short, we don't start the cycle of mercy, because we cannot. Left to our own devices we have no resources or capacity to do so. But God has shown us mercy. In the cross of Christ, he has met us in our need—he has had compassion on us and forgiven us our sins. We need mercy to enter into his kingdom, and we continue to need his mercy as we go on in the Christian life. Our spiritual poverty has been turned around, but we are never beyond the need for God's mercy.

Because of this, we are to show mercy to those around us—and not with limits, and long memories. True mercy does not keep count (18:21-35). Possibly to underscore the point, Jesus does not speak of a person doing individual acts of mercy that can be tallied up, but of a person who is 'merciful'. A person characterised by mercy.

As members of God's kingdom, we are to be like our king. He is merciful and gracious, slow to anger, and abounding in steadfast love and faithfulness, forgiving iniquity and transgression and sin (Exodus 34:6-7. Ephesians 2:4-5). If he has shown us such great mercy, how can we deny mercy to others? How can we be unforgiving? How can we be harsh and impatient with those who sin? How can we disregard those who are in need?

Such mercy does not arise from the hope of receiving a return. That would not be mercy at all. Rather, the mercy we extend in generous forgiveness to those who have hurt us or in heartfelt compassion to those in need, is both a recognition of our own need, and a response to the boundless mercy we ourselves have received from the God of all mercies.

Questions for Reflection

1. In what ways has God shown mercy to you?
2. In what ways have you received mercy from others?
3. How might you show mercy to others? In particular, are there certain relationships where your mercy is overdue?

Prayer
Merciful God,
thank you that you are gracious and kind,
slow to anger, and abounding in love.
You do not treat us as our sins deserve but you forgive
us generously and graciously, and mercifully give us
everything we need.
Please renew our hearts by your Holy Spirit
so we might live lives characterised by your mercy,
showing forgiveness to those who sin against us
and compassion to those in need.
May the overflowing mercy of our lives bring honour
to you, the God who is rich in mercy. Amen.

Claire Smith is a New Testament scholar and women's Bible teacher. She and her husband Rob are members of St Andrew's Cathedral, Sydney, Australia.

6. Pure Vision

Now if the ministry that brought death, which was engraved in letters on stone, came with glory, so that the Israelites could not look steadily at the face of Moses because of its glory, transitory though it was, will not the ministry of the Spirit be even more glorious? If the ministry that brought condemnation was glorious, how much more glorious is the ministry that brings righteousness! For what was glorious has no glory now in comparison with the surpassing glory. And if what was transitory came with glory, how much greater is the glory of that which lasts!

Therefore, since we have such a hope, we are very bold. We are not like Moses, who would put a veil over his face to prevent the Israelites from seeing the end of what was passing away. But their minds were made dull, for to this day the same veil remains when the old covenant is read. It has not been removed, because only in Christ is it taken away. Even to this day when Moses is read, a veil covers their hearts. But whenever anyone turns to the Lord, the veil is taken away. Now the Lord is the Spirit, and where the Spirit of the Lord is, there is freedom. And we all, who with unveiled faces contemplate the Lord's glory, are being transformed into his image with ever-increasing glory, which comes from the Lord, who is the Spirit.

Starter Question
How can we come to God?

TODAY'S TEXT
Blessed are the pure in heart, for they will see God.
Matthew 5:8

When Moses went up Mount Sinai to receive the Ten Commandments, he saw God. It had an extraordinary effect on him. Some of God's glory rubbed off, and his face shone brightly.

Strontium aluminate is a phosphorescent material. It absorbs radiation and then emits it slowly at a lower intensity. After a few hours in daylight, it glows in the dark. It's not something that usually happens to human skin, although some sunscreens are phosphorescent.

Moses's face shone so brightly that it was blinding. It was like looking at the sun, or at car headlights. In 2 Corinthians 3, Paul says that the old law is like that. Like a bright light in a cellar, it shows up all the dirt and muck that has accumulated in our hearts and lives. It shows God's perfect goodness and righteousness, and so it shows our evil ways and rebellion against him. We can't look at it, because it is too painful.

LIFTING THE VEIL
Jesus blesses the pure in heart with the sight of God. Yet, in the same way as the merciful who receive mercy were shown mercy first (verse 7), it is a cycle that begins with his gracious intervention. Those who see God will be made pure in heart, by seeing him.

If the old law can have this effect on Moses and the people of Israel, how much more will the ministry of the Spirit affect Paul and the church of Corinth? God's glory revealed in the law made Moses's face shine. How much more will God's glory revealed in Christ make the ministry of Paul and the life of the church shine?

Moses' face dazzled the people, so he had to wear a veil until it wore off. Paul used Moses as a picture to explain his ministry to the church in Corinth. A veil covers the heart of those under the old covenant, because their hearts are not pure. 'Whenever anyone turns to the Lord, the veil is taken away.' Then something wonderful happens, 'We, who with unveiled faces all reflect the Lord's glory, are being transformed into his likeness with ever-increasing glory, which comes from the Lord, who is the Spirit.'

When we come to Christ the barrier between us and God is removed; the veil on our hearts is lifted. All our proud rejection of God's rule that stops us from saying yes to God. All our self-centred thinking that blocks out God's voice. All our bitterness that blackens God's name because we feel we deserve better. It's all lifted.

Like a blindfold being removed we can suddenly see God in his glory, his holiness, his beauty, his love, his mercy, his grace and his power. We are free to gaze on his glory. As John Piper wrote, "The ultimate good of the gospel is seeing and savouring the beauty and value of God." [John Piper, *God is the Gospel* (Leicester: IVP, 2005), 56]

A TRANSFORMING VISION

Just as the glory of God made Moses's face shine, so, as we gaze on the glory of God we are changed; we are transformed into his likeness. This is the new covenant. It is not a law engraved in stone, that sets a standard we can never attain. It is the Holy Spirit at work in our hearts, changing us so we reflect the image of God.

Jesus took away the veil—our rejection of God—by taking it on himself, as if it were his, and bearing God's judgment on it. We get a new start, a new relationship with God based on what Christ has done for us. This is the new deal, the new agreement, the new covenant. A new relationship with God based on the word of Christ. The pure in heart will see God.

As we hear the beautiful truth of the new covenant from the whole of scripture, the Spirit writes a letter of Christ on the hearts of his people. As we see his goodness and love shine out of our church family, we are looking into his face and seeing his glory, and so he changes our hearts to love him more.

QUESTIONS FOR REFLECTION

1. What thrills you about seeing God?
2. How has God purified your heart?
3. How has God changed you to love him more?

PRAYER

God of glory and grace,
you brought us to behold the beauty of
your holiness with unveiled faces
through the new covenant in the blood of Christ:
transform us into his likeness with
ever increasing glory
that our hearts may be pure,
and our lives reflect your holiness,
by the power of the Holy Spirit
and in the name of Jesus,
Amen.

George Crowder *is a Regional Director of Church Society and vicar of St John's, Over.*

7. Peacemaking Children

Bible Reading
Matthew 5:43-48

You have heard that it was said, 'Love your neighbour and hate your enemy.' But I tell you, love your enemies and pray for those who persecute you, that you may be children of your Father in heaven. He causes his sun to rise on the evil and the good, and sends rain on the righteous and the unrighteous. If you love those who love you, what reward will you get? Are not even the tax collectors doing that? And if you greet only your own people, what are you doing more than others? Do not even pagans do that? Be perfect, therefore, as your heavenly Father is perfect.

Starter Question
What is the deepest kind of peace?

Today's Text
Blessed are the peacemakers,
for they will be called children of God.
Matthew 5:9

Why should the peacemakers be called children or, more literally, "sons of God"? It's quite a claim. To have the kingdom of heaven, to be comforted or to inherit the earth is one thing, but to be called "sons of God" is quite another. It almost sounds blasphemous. What is Jesus getting at?

Ah, someone might say, in the Bible to be a "son of" someone means that you share their character. That same someone might point out that Jesus himself gave James and John the nickname "sons of thunder" (Mark 3:17) and that when Jesus was not received by a Samaritan village these same two brothers asked him "Lord, do you want us to tell fire to come down from heaven and consume them?" (Luke 9:54). Pretty thunderous stuff. That is, of course, true. But to be called a son of God means that you act in a divine manner, and that is still a pretty extraordinary claim. What is it about peacemakers which earns them this most exalted title?

The Great Peacemaker
To get at an answer, perhaps we might start with *the* Son of God. When Isaiah prophesied the birth of Christ, he spoke of him as the "Prince of Peace" and went on to state that "of the increase of his government and of peace there will be no end" (Isaiah 9:6-7). Micah looked forward to a ruler who would come out of Bethlehem and, the prophet continued, "he shall be their peace" (Micah 5:2,5).

Jesus, then, is the great Prince of Peace, the great peacemaker. The peace he comes to bring is a deep peace indeed. It is reconciliation with God, not simply a lack of war. It is restoring the sinner's relationship with God, not just carving out a bit of quiet. As the Apostle Paul reminds us, Jesus "came and preached peace to you who were far off and peace to those who were near. For through him we both have access in one Spirit to the Father" (Ephesians 2:17–18). Jew or Gentile, Christ came to make us one and to bring peace.

Like Father, Like Son

To be a peacemaker, then, is to be Christlike. We can be "sons of God" because we are like the Son of God. Male or female, when you place all your hope and trust in Christ you are "in Christ". You are part of the "Body of Christ". You "have come to share in Christ" (Hebrews 3:14), and so you share in his Sonship. You receive "the Spirit of his Son" (Galatians 4:6), and so you can cry out "Abba Father". You are an heir! You are "joined to the Lord" and "become one spirit with him" (1 Corinthians 6:17). As we place our faith in Christ, we also share in his Sonship. And so we are peacemakers.

But how? How do you put all of this into practice? How can you be a peacemaker at 11:30am on a Thursday morning? A little later on in the Sermon on the Mount Jesus gives us an example of just one step we could take, a place to start. He says: "love your enemies and pray for those who persecute you, so that you may be sons of your Father who is in heaven" (Matthew 5:44–45). Peacemaking begins at home and at work. The peacemaker is the one who loves his or her enemies. The peacemaker is the one who responds to being persecuted by praying for the persecutor.

From the cross, the great Prince of Peace prayed for those who executed him: "Father, forgive them, for they know not what they do" (Luke 23:34). As Stephen, a son of God and the first Christian martyr, died he fell to his knees and uttered his final words: "Lord, do not hold this sin against them" (Acts 7:60).

Blessed indeed are the peacemakers! Truly they are sons of God.

QUESTIONS FOR REFLECTION

1. How can sharing the gospel itself make you into a peacemaker?
2. If you were to pray for those who persecute you (or the church), who would be the first person to come to mind?
3. How might you experience the peace of Christ, even when in great difficulty?

PRAYER

Almighty Father,
who sent your only-begotten Son
to reconcile all who trust in him to yourself:
strengthen us to reflect his peace to those around us,
and to pray for those who persecute us,
that all may know that through Christ
salvation is found
and a reconciliation with you may be gained,
through our Lord and Saviour Jesus Christ
who is the long hoped for Prince of Peace,
Amen.

Chris Moore *is the rector of a rural, multi-parish benefice in the Diocese of Hereford and Regional Director of Church Society in the West Midlands and South West of England.*

8. Blessed Persecuted

Bible Reading
Acts 7:59-8:8

While they were stoning him, Stephen prayed, 'Lord Jesus, receive my spirit.' Then he fell on his knees and cried out, 'Lord, do not hold this sin against them.' When he had said this, he fell asleep. And Saul approved of their killing him. On that day a great persecution broke out against the church in Jerusalem, and all except the apostles were scattered throughout Judea and Samaria. Godly men buried Stephen and mourned deeply for him. But Saul began to destroy the church. Going from house to house, he dragged off both men and women and put them in prison. Those who had been scattered preached the word wherever they went. Philip went down to a city in Samaria and proclaimed the Messiah there. When the crowds heard Philip and saw the signs he performed, they all paid close attention to what he said. For with shrieks, impure spirits came out of many, and many who were paralysed or lame were healed. So there was great joy in that city.

Starter Question
Does persecution bring benefits? If so, what?

Today's Text

Blessed are those who are persecuted for righteousness'
sake, for theirs is the kingdom of heaven.
Matthew 5:10

For the last thirty years or so, Northern Nigeria, where I
live, has seen a series of riots, persecutions, and destruction.
Sometimes whole families or communities are decimated;
sometimes it is individuals who just happen to be in the wrong
place at the wrong time, and who refused to deny Christ, choosing rather to be killed. In the vast majority of instances the names
of these martyrs will be known and remembered only by their
close relatives—and by the Lord. Some were those who were working for peace and reconciliation between Muslims and Christians;
some were pastors; many were ordinary church members.

No-one in their right mind actually wants persecution; persecution is something which we work to eliminate. Modern trans-
lations which render Matthew 5:10 as "Happy are you who are
persecuted" may encourage a dangerously wrong interpretation of
Christian faith and practice. Suffering and persecution do not ensure a safe passage to heaven! We should not look for suffering. We
must debunk the idea that passively accepting a state of suffering
is a sign of being a believer.

Inevitable opposition

Persecution and suffering are, however, part of life. God has
never promised his people that they would escape all trouble, but
he has always promised to go through the troubles with us. This is
clear even in the Old Testament:

But now, this is what the LORD says—
  he who created you, Jacob,
  he who formed you, Israel:
"Do not fear, for I have redeemed you;
  I have summoned you by name; you are mine.

When you pass through the waters,
　　I will be with you;
and when you pass through the rivers,
　　they will not sweep over you.
When you walk through the fire,
　　you will not be burned;
　　the flames will not set you ablaze.　　*Isaiah 43:1-2*

Jesus himself reinforces this not only with the promise that he will always be with his people, but also that his power has been proved greater than any evil. He said: 'In this world you will have trouble ['face persecution', NRSV]. But take heart! I have overcome the world' (John 16:33).

In the New Testament and throughout the years since then it has been clear that those who carry the message of the gospel will not always be welcomed; there will be intimidation, persecution, humiliation, and suffering. St. Paul, for example, knew all of these, but he refused to give up. Always, under all circumstances, his reason for living was to 'press on' with the gospel (Philippians 3:12).

Spreading the word

Stephen was one of the seven deacons appointed by the apostles to help with the administration and running of the early church. Stephen, however, was also a gifted preacher and teacher, and his bold and faithful ministry aroused such hatred that he was arrested and condemned to death. Thereafter persecution increased against all the Christians. One effect of this was that the Christians scattered, and of course they took their faith with them. In this way the gospel spread over a wide area, and more and more people eagerly listened as the gospel was proclaimed and explained to them. The gospel was moving on, and many responded—no matter the cost.

Still today, in various countries and situations many who come forward for baptism, do so knowing that they will be turned out of their homes, disowned by their family and abused by their former friends. It was to meet such a situation that Peter wrote his first letter to reassure and to bring hope to those who were beginning to face the storms of persecution. The letter instructs us and points us to the basis of our faith, Jesus Christ, our hope, now and for ever. Peter points to the glory of God's calling: Christians are God's chosen people, heirs of God's blessing—but Christians are also called to suffer, to endure unjust abuse and undeserved persecution. This is our calling because it was Christ's calling, and we are called to follow his example (1 Peter 2:21). Christ suffered for our sake, and as we follow him, we suffer for his sake and for the sake of bringing others to know him.

QUESTIONS FOR REFLECTION

1. How can persecution strengthen our faith?
2. How are persecution and evangelism linked? Can you think of examples from the Bible and from today?
3. In Acts 7:59-8:8, what do you think was the effect of Stephen's death on (a) the church (b) the opponents of the gospel?

PRAYER
Almighty and most merciful Father,
whose Son Jesus Christ suffered pain, abuse, and death
that we might know freedom, joy, and life:
Strengthen those who are suffering for the gospel now,
and grant to all your people such trust in you
that we may faithfully serve you in this life
and finally be with you in the kingdom of heaven.
Grant this for the sake of your Son, our Saviour Jesus Christ,
Amen.

Benjamin Kwashi is the Bishop of Jos in Nigeria and General Secretary of GAFCON

9. SLANDERED REWARDED

BIBLE READING
1 Peter 4:12-19

Dear friends, do not be surprised at the fiery ordeal that has come on you to test you, as though something strange were happening to you. But rejoice inasmuch as you participate in the sufferings of Christ, so that you may be overjoyed when his glory is revealed. If you are insulted because of the name of Christ, you are blessed, for the Spirit of glory and of God rests on you. If you suffer, it should not be as a murderer or thief or any other kind of criminal, or even as a meddler. However, if you suffer as a Christian, do not be ashamed, but praise God that you bear that name. For it is time for judgment to begin with God's household; and if it begins with us, what will the outcome be for those who do not obey the gospel of God? And,

"If it is hard for the righteous to be saved,

what will become of the ungodly and the sinner?"

So then, those who suffer according to God's will should commit themselves to their faithful Creator and continue to do good.

STARTER QUESTION
What injustice or misunderstanding have you suffered that you could not remedy, and how did you respond?

Today's Text

Blessed are you when people insult you, persecute you
and falsely say all kinds of evil against you because of
me. Rejoice and be glad, because great is your reward
in heaven, for in the same way they persecuted the
prophets who were before you.
Matthew 5:11-12

I sat in front of my computer in stunned disbelief. A person with
whom I have had friendly online encounters discovered that I
am human after all. I hadn't responded to her over some online
spat (not mine, but hers and another person's) in the way she had
expected me to. Her cutting salvo, 'You're just like everyone else,'
resounded across my bruised feelings. I read back over our heated,
and on my part, defensive exchange. And yet, I wasn't wrong, I just
hadn't been the person she wanted me to be. I sought counsel from
wiser Christians. 'So,' said an unpleasantly discerning one, 'why do
you have to have everyone like you?' And then he added, 'Blessed
are you when others revile you', before walking away.

A Christian, in an abstract sense, knows that persecution is part
of the deal. Jesus promised that the road would be narrow and
hard, that the way of the cross is the way of life, putting together
two contradictory ideas—death (the cross), and life (not death).
But against that abstract knowledge is the deep, pervasive desire to
be kind, which often masks the desire to be liked. Persecution is
something that happens out there, in other places, to people who
are really suffering. If it's small, or mediocre, or mundane, it probably wouldn't merit any great reward.

Divine perspective

The Beatitudes, however, of which this might be considered the
crowning glory, are not a list of commandments to obey. They are
not the Christian's divinely ordained To-Do list. They are descrip-
tive pronouncements from the vantage point of heaven. The meek,

the peaceful, the hungry, the merciful, the mourning, and yes, even the persecuted are all blessed by God. God gives to his children gifts associated with his attentive favour. Looking at these gifts from the world's point of view, the recipients are wretched and despised. From God's perspective, however, they are of all the most fortunate.

Moreover, it is not the elite Christian alone who may expect to receive the blessings of persecution. Persecution for the sake of the gospel is for every believer, whether in intense waves, as is the case in China, South Korea, and Nigeria today, or in the pitiful painful broken relationships that are the property of being a Christian in an ever more secularised West.

'Do not be surprised,' admonishes Peter, precisely because the Christians to whom he was writing were surprised, and sad, that life was so difficult, 'as if something strange were happening to you.' He has to say it, because it is so strange. The Christian, having experienced a deep, settled peace with God, having been forgiven an incalculable debt, turns to the world, happy and secure, and is then shocked when the world recoils in horror.

And recoil it will, because though Jesus accomplished the profound peace of reconciliation for the believer to God on the cross, yet he has not come again in glory. His kingdom resides alongside the kingdom of this world, of death, of the enemy of the soul. This great enemy, though he has lost, is out to do as much damage as he can on his ultimate descent into hell.

Martin Luther describes it this way in his commentary on the Sermon on the Mount: 'There neither can nor ought to be a peaceful, quiet state of things. For how could it be so where the devil is ruling, and is a deadly enemy to the gospel? And this, indeed, not without reason, for it hurts him in his kingdom, so that he feels it… Therefore, do not hope for any peace and quietness as long as Christ and his gospel are in the midst of the devil's kingdom.'

GOSPEL LIGHT

The key is not to go looking for persecution, to be obnoxious on purpose and then claim it was all for Jesus. Nor is it to retreat from all interaction with the world. Rather, it is to take every circumstance in which you thought you were acting in good faith and with sincere charity of heart, every painful misunderstanding, every time you discovered you were deeply at odds with those around you, and bring each one under the light of the gospel.

Sometimes that light will humble you, when you realize that you were the persecutor, you were wrong, you must go back and try to reconcile. But other times you will discover that you longed for peace with the world over peace with God, that your idea of kindness was a desire to avoid conflict, or worse, that Jesus offers you a taste of the suffering of the cross—that strange, life-giving, disquieting entrance into a great and beautiful reward.

QUESTIONS FOR REFLECTION

1. How do you respond to suffering in general? Are you surprised? Anxious? Joyful?
2. How do you respond to being in the wrong? Are you swift to seek forgiveness? Or swift to retrench your position?
3. How do you pray for yourself when you suffer persecution, and others around the world?

PRAYER
Holy and Merciful God,
whose blessed Son went willingly to the suffering of the cross
that we might find it the way of life:
give us grace to rejoice in every suffering,
that we might see how great is our reward in heaven,
through Jesus Christ our Saviour, *Amen.*

Anne Kennedy blogs about current events and theological trends at Preventing Grace, a blog on Patheos.com and is the author of Nailed It: 365 Devotions for Angry or Worn-Out People.

the
FRUIT OF
THE SPIRIT

10. LOVE

BIBLE READING
2 Peter 1:5-9

For this very reason, make every effort to add to your faith goodness; and to goodness, knowledge; and to knowledge, self-control; and to self-control, perseverance; and to perseverance, godliness; and to godliness, mutual affection; and to mutual affection, love. For if you possess these qualities in increasing measure, they will keep you from being ineffective and unproductive in your knowledge of our Lord Jesus Christ. But whoever does not have them is nearsighted and blind, forgetting that they have been cleansed from their past sins.

STARTER QUESTION
How do we become more Christ-like in our lives in order to bring glory to God and be a faithful witness to Jesus Christ in this world?

Today's Text

But the fruit of the Spirit is love, joy, peace, forbearance,
kindness, goodness, faithfulness, gentleness and self-
control. Against such things there is no law.
Galatians 5:22-23

The apostle Paul teaches us that a Christ-like character bears
the fruit of the Spirit. This, he tells us, is love, joy, peace,
forbearance, kindness, goodness, faithfulness, gentleness,
self-control.

I have always found it important to remind myself and others
that these nine qualities of Galatians chapter 5 form one single
fruit. They are not nine unconnected or different kinds of fruit.
The nine qualities of the fruit of the Spirit form one, ready to be
plucked, perfectly ripened fruit in the life of every believer in Jesus
Christ. As this happens, Jesus shines through our lives and brings
light into the dark places of this world.

Cultivating the fruit of the Spirit has its challenges! It can sometimes be easier to cultivate love than it is to exercise self-control.
In the same way, it can appear more achievable to be faithful than
it is to be gentle. And yet, as the minister who led my ordination
retreat said, if there is one portion of the fruit of the Spirit missing
in your life, you are in crisis! The minister was correct. There is a
dramatic void in the life of a Christian if we are not blossoming
with the full and complete fruit of the Spirit.

Producing fruit

So then, how are we to produce this fruit of the Spirit?

Fruitfulness means Christ-likeness. Fruit is every evidence of
the authentic life of Jesus in us which marks us as belonging to
him and living for him in our time and in our culture, however
difficult that may be.

In John's Gospel, Jesus himself speaks much about fruit. In

chapter 15, He says, 'If you remain in me and I in you, you will bear much fruit; apart from me you can do nothing' (John 15:5). The key to bearing fruit is to abide in Jesus. And the place we go to learn how to abide in him and blossom with the fruit of the Spirit is the word of God. It is there in the word of God we find the wisdom we need to cultivate the fruit of the Spirit and grow in Christ-likeness.

For example, if you have a tendency to speak and react too quickly, reflecting on the word of God will be helpful to you as you cultivate self-control. Consider Proverbs 17:27-28, 'The one who has knowledge uses words with restraint, and whoever has understanding is even-tempered. Even fools are thought wise if they keep silent, and discerning if they hold their tongues.' Elsewhere in the Bible we are taught to give thanks in all circumstances; for this is the will of God in Christ Jesus for you (1 Thessalonians 5:18). Giving thanks in both the good and the difficult days of our lives helps us to produce the goodness and faithfulness which Paul asserts are essential qualities in the life of every Christian.

THE FRUIT OF LOVE

Particularly today, what of cultivating *love*, without which we are nothing? Again, going to the Bible and abiding in the word of God will assist us in cultivating the fruit of the Spirit. In 1 Corinthians 13 we read, 'Love bears all things, believes all things, hopes all things, endures all things. Love never ends.' And in his first letter, John reminds us that 'This is how we know what love is: Jesus Christ laid down his life for us. And we ought to lay down our lives for our brothers and sisters' (1 John 3:16).

We go to the Bible, not just to read and meditate on the word of God, but to discover Jesus in whom we find the fulness of the fruit of the Spirit. God is love, and it is in him that we discover the liberating truth about love; his love for us in that while we were still sinners, Christ died for us (Romans 5:8). As we read about his love for the disciples, we also discover a Saviour who is patient, kind, and good. To a woman caught in a terrible sin, we discover Jesus is gentle. He models self-control as he is falsely accused before the Jewish leaders, and there on the cross, as he gave up his life for us, we learn about his faithfulness to the will of God no matter what the cost.

Jesus said, 'a tree is recognised by its fruit' (Matthew 12:33). May we be known as those who blossom with the fulness of the fruit of the Spirit in order that we might glorify God in our daily lives.

QUESTIONS FOR REFLECTION

1. Which aspect of the fruit of the Spirit do you find the most difficult to cultivate?
2. How can you grow in these areas?
3. Ask someone who knows you well to reflect on the fruit of the Spirit in your life. Where do I have strength? Where do I need to grow? Give thanks to God for the areas of strength and pray with them in the areas of growth.

PRAYER
Almighty and everlasting God,
we come to you in the name of your Son:
grant that we, like him, may blossom with the fulness
of the fruit of the Spirit,
so that our lives will bring glory to you
and radiate with the beauty of your presence,
through Jesus Christ, God with us,
our only mediator and advocate,
who radiates for us the perfect portrait of God,
Amen.

Julian Dobbs is the Bishop of the Anglican Diocese of the Living Word (USA).

11. Joy

Bible Reading
1 Peter 1:3-9

Praise be to the God and Father of our Lord Jesus Christ! In his great mercy he has given us new birth into a living hope through the resurrection of Jesus Christ from the dead, and into an inheritance that can never perish, spoil or fade. This inheritance is kept in heaven for you, who through faith are shielded by God's power until the coming of the salvation that is ready to be revealed in the last time. In all this you greatly rejoice, though now for a little while you may have had to suffer grief in all kinds of trials. These have come so that the proven genuineness of your faith—of greater worth than gold, which perishes even though refined by fire—may result in praise, glory and honour when Jesus Christ is revealed. Though you have not seen him, you love him; and even though you do not see him now, you believe in him and are filled with an inexpressible and glorious joy, for you are receiving the end result of your faith, the salvation of your souls.

Starter Question
When are you full of joy?

Today's Text

But the fruit of the Spirit is love, joy, peace, forbearance, kindness, goodness, faithfulness, gentleness and self-control. Against such things there is no law.

Galatians 5:22-23

Walking onto the veranda of our church building, I see Kay standing by the entrance door smiling with genuine interest as she talks to another beside her. I smile to both ladies as I head towards the door, but Kay stops me to ask for a brief update about a particular ministry matter. I see a brightness and keenness as she listens and then responds, 'I'll continue praying.'

There is nothing extraordinary about this meeting, except that as I walk into the hall, I find myself thankful for her, with tears in my eyes. She has ridden the waves of grief and pain in both distant and recent years, while her body fails her that bit more each day; yet, she is able to be constant in her praise and thankfulness to God with an undeniable steadfastness. There are some days when her sadness and struggle are visible, yet a warm brightness remains on her face and in her voice. Upon meeting Kay, one cannot miss that she is full of a joy that increases rather than diminishes. When asked how she remains joyful, her voice quivered as she said, 'Because I am able to remember what I have in him.'

Joy in suffering

Kay's response is shaped by 1 Peter 1:3–9. In this passage, Peter is writing to Christian believers who have been scattered across the Roman empire because their conviction about the Lordship of Jesus clashed with Roman ideology. Having been forced out of homes, with livelihoods lost, they were well acquainted with suffering. Peter lifts their eyes from their present earthly circumstances to their eternal reality shaped by who they are in Christ and their future hope in him. However, as Peter writes to these believers, his words are also preserved for us; we too are believers living in a world where we do not belong and which does not want us, because of whom we represent.

Peter focuses upon who we are through the death and resurrection of the Lord Jesus. Because of the generous kindness of God the Father, we have a new birth through dying and rising in Christ. A new birth means a new social identity where our Father is the same Father as the Lord Jesus Christ's and we together belong to God's household. Having a new status, we are invited to share in the inheritance of the firstborn—the Lord Jesus—who is the first to rise from the dead. This inheritance is more than certain, it is unspoiled. Not even the decay of our earthly world can ruin this inheritance because our life in Christ, and our future in him, does not belong to this earthly domain of our present circumstances, but rather our inheritance belongs to the eternal domain of God's kingdom.

This is not unimaginable; it is our present and future reality in the Lord Jesus. Irrespective of what happens in our everyday lives, circumstances cannot change or diminish who we are in Christ now or our eternal future with him. By expressing this beautiful reality as praise, Peter reminds us that who we are and what we have in Christ is dependent upon the generous mercy and kindness of our Father; we have contributed nothing to being born anew into our Father's household with its glorious inheritance – it is entirely him.

For this reason, Peter reminds us that we can continue to have joy—that fruit of the Spirit—irrespective of how tough and painful our external and earthly circumstances are. Peter is referring not only to suffering caused by persecution but 'all kinds of trials.' These trials could be the loss of health or physical mobility, the struggles of doing life as a family in a broken world, the loss of a job, the loss of a life cut short or before the life was born, the ugliness of death and our rebellion against God, or from the constant pressure to conform our beliefs to the culture in which we live.

Peter is not saying that we are impervious to pain and suffering, but rather that these trials are for the short-term, relative to our eternal future with Christ.

Joy in hope

By being preserved through trials, our trust in Jesus is refined, with all the dross and impurities being separated from our faith and then destroyed. What is left, is genuine. While painful, Peter says that the riches of knowing that our faith in Jesus is being purified is a cause for praise, glory, and honour at the return of Christ. This honour is not now, but a delayed honour.

Our cause for joy and rejoicing now is not a reaction to our present circumstances. Yet we know internally, through the presence of the Spirit, that the praise and glory at the return of Christ is worth more than any earthly riches can hold for us now. While we wait for Jesus's return, having never seen him face-to-face, we continue to love and trust him, which are two internal convictions that we steadfastly cling to and cherish. By remembering who we are and what we have in Jesus, our joy is glorious and extends beyond words because we hold firmly onto a glorious and living hope—we are saved to life eternal with our Lord.

Questions for Reflection

1. What is the difference between joy and happiness for the Christian believer?
2. How are you holding fast to the great mercy that God our Father has demonstrated to us in Christ, in your present circumstances?
3. Where do you see evidence in your own life of being filled with a glorious joy that is beyond words because of the salvation you have in Christ?

PRAYER

Our God and Father,
you have shown such generous kindness to us,
giving us a new birth through the death and
resurrection of Jesus,
and a living hope of an imperishable inheritance.
Although we have not seen our Lord Jesus,
we love him and believe in him.
In your mercy, continue to preserve and refine our
faith through every kind of trial,
that our faith may be purified and proven genuine.
Sustain in us an inexpressible and glorious joy
through Jesus Christ our Saviour,
Amen.

Katy Smith *is the Principal of Mary Andrews College in Sydney, Australia.*

12. PEACE

Romans 5:1-5

Therefore, since we have been justified through faith, we have peace with God through our Lord Jesus Christ, through whom we have gained access by faith into this grace in which we now stand. And we boast in the hope of the glory of God. Not only so, but we also glory in our sufferings, because we know that suffering produces perseverance; perseverance, character; and character, hope. And hope does not put us to shame, because God's love has been poured out into our hearts through the Holy Spirit, who has been given to us.

STARTER QUESTION

In what situations or circumstances have you found your relationships with other believers under huge pressure or fracturing?

TODAY'S TEXT
But the fruit of the Spirit is love, joy, peace, forbearance, kindness, goodness, faithfulness, gentleness and self-|control. Against such things there is no law.
Galatians 5:22-23

I googled 'spirituality' and discovered that there is no widely agreed definition. One scholar said that in his research he discovered 27 options, most of which had nothing in common. In Galatians 5:16-25 spirituality is on view, or more specifically, the work of the Holy Spirit in a believer's life. The disciple of Jesus will 'walk by the Spirit', be 'led by the Spirit' and produce 'the fruit of the Spirit.' God's Spirit and our flesh (sinful nature) are in conflict—the latter displaying sinful results and the former producing fruit that is Christ-like. In this chapter, we are going to focus on one characteristic of the work of the Holy Spirit in the life of a believer, namely, peace.

PEACE IN GALATIA
Apart from Galatians 5:22, peace is mentioned two other times in the letter. In both instances, it is to do with our relationship with God. In Galatians 1:3-4 we read '… peace to you from God our Father and the Lord Jesus Christ, who gave himself for our sins to rescue us.' Jesus died on our behalf to deal with the wrath God rightly has towards us—to establish peace between us and God. Then, in Galatians 6:14-16 we are told that we have peace with God if we boast in the cross of Christ and don't rely on religious rules. Peace is equated with the fulness of our salvation. The great old hymn 'It is well with my soul' captures this well when it says:

> *My sin, oh, the bliss of this glorious thought*
> *My sin, not in part but the whole,*
> *Is nailed to the cross and I bear it no more,*
> *Praise the Lord, praise the Lord, o my soul.*

However, the context here in Galatians 5 indicates that the peace on view is not just a Godward matter but also has application to our relationships with other Christians. Earlier, in Galatians 5, we are instructed to 'serve one another humbly in love' (verse 13) and not to 'bite and devour each other' (verse 15). The acts of the flesh in verses 19-21 destroy the relationships between believers. In Galatians 5:20 'discord' is listed as a sinful act of the flesh. It is to be quarrelsome and cause strife with brothers and sisters in Christ. Discord is the opposite of the peace being referred to in Galatians 5:22. Acts of the flesh stop people inheriting the kingdom of God, but they also destroy the fellowship of believers. In contrast, the fruit of the Spirit is evidence of salvation and builds united and loving Christian communities.

More specifically and positively what will this peace look like? It is to focus on the salvation we have in common and the outworking of this. As the Spirit produces in us all 9 characteristics/fruit mentioned in Galatians 5:22-23, we experience peace. It also means avoiding controversies and squabbles about non-central issues like preferred styles of services, church music, and denominational idiosyncrasies. Instead we are to so value the relationships we have in Christ that we strive to love one another and avoid anything that would destroy this bond.

FIGHTING FOR PEACE

However, Galatians does not advocate a 'peace at all cost' approach. Interestingly, the letter highlights the conflict that the Apostle Paul has with a number of people. In Galatians 2:11 Paul says that 'When Cephas (Peter) came to Antioch I opposed him to his face.' At the start of chapter 3 he says to the believers in Galatia "You foolish Galatians!' (he missed the seminar on how to win friends and influence people). In chapter 5 he speaks about those who are trying to lead the Galatians back into observing the Old Testament law in less than polite terms: 'As for those agitators, I wish they would go the whole way and emasculate themselves!' It doesn't seem like a very peace-generating approach.

At this point Paul is being totally consistent with his gospel convictions. He knows that a person only has peace with God by trusting in the atoning sacrifice of the Lord Jesus. Any tampering with the gospel of grace undercuts all this. So, Paul will always 'fight' for the gospel of 'peace' even if it means engaging in conflict. I suspect that the risk for twenty-first century western believers is that we will fight over the non-central matters and avoid the tough arguments about central gospel truths such as the atoning death of Christ or continuing sin that will exclude people from the kingdom of God.

God is at work in us by his Spirit to convict us of the peace he has won for us in Christ at the cross. One clear outworking of the Holy Spirit will be to produce peace among brothers and sisters in Christ, but not at the expense of the gospel. One indication of an authentic spiritual church will be the way in which its members strive to pursue what makes for peace.

Questions for Reflection
1. What steps could you take to grow in your understanding of the 'peace' that God has won for you in Christ?
2. When do you think it is appropriate for you to have significant tension with other believers (even though we are called to peace)?
3. Is there sin in your own life or the life of the church you belong to which is creating discord rather than peace? How are we to 'walk by the Spirit' in these situations?

PRAYER

Heavenly Father,
thank you for the grace and peace we have
because the Lord Jesus has given himself for us
on the cross
to rescue us from our sins.
Thank you for the freedom we have in Christ.
By the power of your Holy Spirit,
please help us to live in this freedom,
not to indulge our sinful flesh
but to walk by the Spirit.
Please produce the fruit of the Spirit in our lives.
Confirm in us the peace you have won for us in Christ
and lead us to be those who are peacemakers.
We ask all this in the name of the Lord Jesus,
the Lord of peace,
Amen.

Paul Harrington *is the Rector of Holy Trinity Adelaide and the Senior Pastor of the Trinity Network of Churches in South Australia.*

13. PATIENCE

BIBLE READING
James 5:7-11

Be patient, then, brothers and sisters, until the Lord's coming. See how the farmer waits for the land to yield its valuable crop, patiently waiting for the autumn and spring rains. You too, be patient and stand firm, because the Lord's coming is near. Don't grumble against one another, brothers and sisters, or you will be judged. The Judge is standing at the door!

Brothers and sisters, as an example of patience in the face of suffering, take the prophets who spoke in the name of the Lord. As you know, we count as blessed those who have persevered. You have heard of Job's perseverance and have seen what the Lord finally brought about. The Lord is full of compassion and mercy.

STARTER QUESTION
What do the patience of a farmer, of the prophets, and of Job have to do with us waiting for Jesus to return?

TODAY'S TEXT
But the fruit of the Spirit is love, joy, peace, forbearance,
kindness, goodness, faithfulness, gentleness and self-
control. Against such things there is no law.
Galatians 5:22-23

Ll good things come to those who wait. It's a well-worn cliché,
often used by parents to teach their children that patience
yields rewards. Patience is a virtue. But it is also a gift. It has
to be, because by nature (as our cultures all demonstrate) we are very
impatient creatures craving instant, immediate gratification.

Because we are children of God, not because of our works but
by faith alone, 'God sent the Spirit of his Son into our hearts' (Galatians 4:6). So the spiritual fruit of patience or forbearance is the
result of God the Holy Spirit himself living and working within us.
He transforms and renews us day by day, from what sin has made us
into his own likeness. It is the promised Spirit's own patience which
germinates and grows within us once we are joined to him.

THE PATIENCE OF GOD
This is great news. Because God's own patience is legendary, ac-
claimed across the universe and throughout the pages of scripture.
He is insistent like a glacier carving out a fjord, or the ocean craft-
ing coastlines of elegant sea arch cathedrals. He perseveres in all
his plans, in redemption as well as in creation. He is persistent
despite our sin. He doesn't give up at the first sign of difficulty or
walk away from the most obstinate obstacles. He is tenacious and
determined in his love for us, never losing his resolve to bless the
world despite centuries upon centuries of sinful human rebellion.
He is purposeful. He presses on. He is patient.

When God declared his name to Moses, he called himself 'The
LORD, the LORD, the compassionate and gracious God, *slow to
anger...*' (Exodus 34:6-7). God put up with his people and their
groaning, moaning ingratitude for 40 years (Acts 13:8). Nehemi-

ah thanked him that for many years he was patient with Israel, warning them repeatedly through the prophets despite their hard-hearted, stiff-necked deafness (Nehemiah 9:30). And think of the patience of Jesus! As Spurgeon says, 'It was mighty patience that could bear to tread this world beneath his feet, and not to crush it, when it so ill-treated its Redeemer.'

Paul urges us not to 'show contempt for the riches of his kindness, forbearance and patience,' because it is 'intended to lead you to repentance' (Romans 2:4). He warns us that in the past 'God, although choosing to show his wrath and make his power known, bore with great patience the objects of his wrath—prepared for destruction' (Romans 9:22). But his patience also means salvation (2 Peter 3:15) as he demonstrated by displaying his immense patience through the salvation of stubborn Saul (1 Timothy 1:16), and as he shows us even now. 'The Lord is not slow in keeping his promise, as some understand slowness,' says Peter, 'Instead he is patient with you, not wanting anyone to perish, but everyone to come to repentance' (2 Peter 3:9). Every day that he holds off the second coming of Christ is proof of God's restraint.

OUR PATIENCE

This is the sort of patience which God the Spirit is growing within believers—Godlike patience. It is the sort of patience which allows us to wait for him and tolerate tricky circumstances. 'Be still before the Lord and wait patiently for him' says Psalm 37:7. The word for waiting patiently there is the Hebrew word *chil*. Resist the temptation to be hotheaded and impatient, and 'do not fret when people succeed in their ways, when they carry out their wicked schemes' (Psalm 37:7). God will act. Trust God and chill.

Be patient with everyone (1 Thessalonians 5:14). Because as the Proverbs say:

- 'Whoever is patient has great understanding, but one who is quick-tempered displays folly' (Proverbs 14:29);

- 'A hot-tempered person stirs up conflict, but the one who is patient calms a quarrel' (15:18);
- 'A person's wisdom yields patience; it is to one's glory to overlook an offence' (19:11);
- 'Through patient a ruler can be persuaded, and a gentle tongue can break a bone' (Proverbs 25:15).

Love is patient (1 Corinthians 13:4) so 'be patient, bearing with one another in love' (Ephesians 4:2). 'Be joyful in hope, patient in affliction, faithful in prayer' says the apostle Paul (Romans 12:12). Just as 'Abraham waited patiently and received what was promised' (Hebrews 6:15), so we are not to be lazy 'but to imitate those who through faith and patience inherit what has been promised' (Hebrews 6:12). It's tempting to take a shortcut. It's tempting to do things our way not God's. It's tempting to grumble and fight, employing the weapons of the world rather than prayer and the word. But 'Better a patient person than a warrior, one with self-control than one who takes a city' (Proverbs 16:32). Patience waits for the promises and prophecies, imitating the prophets (James 5:10) and apostles (2 Timothy 3:10, 4:2).

'Be patient, then, brothers and sisters, until the Lord's coming' (James 5:7). On that day, we will have no need for patience anymore. Because as Augustine said, 'there will be no patience in heaven, since there is no need for it except where evils have to be borne; yet that which we shall obtain by patience will be eternal' (*City of God*, 14.9).

QUESTIONS FOR REFLECTION
1. Can you list the ways in which God has been patient with you?
2. When and how does your impatience tend to show itself?
3. How can the example of the prophets, apostles, and Christ inspire you to be more patient in your particular circumstances?

PRAYER

Compassionate and gracious God,
whose slowness to anger urges us to repent of our sin:
strengthen us with all power, according to your
glorious might,
so that we, who are impatient by nature,
may have the patience of the Spirit
to bear with one another in love,
and endure every trial and temptation,
while we wait for the coming of Christ our Saviour,
in whose name we pray,
Amen.

Lee Gatiss is the Director of Church Society and author of Fight Valiantly: Contending for the Faith in the Bible and in the Church of England.

14. Kindness

At one time we too were foolish, disobedient, deceived and enslaved by all kinds of passions and pleasures. We lived in malice and envy, being hated and hating one another. But when the kindness and love of God our Saviour appeared, he saved us, not because of righteous things we had done, but because of his mercy. He saved us through the washing of rebirth and renewal by the Holy Spirit, whom he poured out on us generously through Jesus Christ our Saviour, so that, having been justified by his grace, we might become heirs having the hope of eternal life.

Starter Question
What is surprising about God's kindness?

Today's Text
But the fruit of the Spirit is love, joy, peace, forbearance, kindness, goodness, faithfulness, gentleness and self-control. Against such things there is no law.
Galatians 5:22-23

A t the start of 2020, Australia was reeling from devastating bush fires that had raged in parts of the eastern states since the previous September. Over 18 million hectares of land were burned, more than 6000 buildings including homes destroyed, and estimates say that one billion native animals and livestock were lost. In addition to communities ravaged by fires, 30 Australians lost their lives including three volunteer fire fighters. In the midst of this catastrophic summer, there were regular stories of the kindness of strangers. People rescuing and caring for native animals; neighbours holding and embracing one another in silent, heartfelt sympathy and support; meals, clothes, toys, and even furniture donated to emergency evacuation centres to assist those who have lost everything. And for weeks on end, millions and millions of dollars were donated to major charities in support of affected communities.

So it may come as a surprise to see the Apostle Paul refer to kindness as a fruit of the Spirit—something requiring the supernatural work of the indwelling Holy Spirit to bring it about in the follower of Jesus.

The kindness of God
The Bible reveals that God is kind. His kindness includes the creation of the world and the gift of life (Job 10:12), but is particularly associated with his mighty and gracious acts of covenant love towards his people: 'I will tell of the kindnesses of the Lord, the deeds for which he is to be praised, according to all the LORD has done for us— yes, the many good things he has done for Israel, according to his compassion and many kindnesses' (Isaiah 63:7).

God's kindness towards Israel is not only a matter of acting powerfully to rescue them, but also his steadfast faithfulness towards them despite their faithlessness. Ultimately, God expresses his saving grace towards an undeserving world in the gift of his Son: '..the incomparable riches of his grace, expressed in his kindness to us in Christ Jesus (Ephesians 2:7). The biblical frame of kindness then, is not merely the acts of compassion that might be observed between sympathetic countrymen in a time of desperate need, but a settled disposition and intention to bless those who neither deserve nor would expect such treatment. So, Jesus teaches his followers to 'love your enemies, do good to them, and lend to them without expecting to get anything back… because (God) is kind to the ungrateful and wicked' (Luke 6:35).

As Paul writes to the church in Galatia, the harmony and fruitfulness of the fellowship of God's people is at risk because some are 'biting and devouring' each other having become 'conceited, provoking and envying each other' (Galatians 5:16, 25). In Colossians, the unity of the fellowship where 'Christ is all and Christ is in all' is the basis for Paul's exhortation to the believers to clothe themselves with kindness (Colossians 3:12), and in Ephesians he urges that Christians 'be kind …to one another, forgiving each other just as in Christ, God forgave you' (Ephesians 4:32).

THE WORK OF THE SPIRIT

Kindness is not a private virtue. It is an essential aspect of love (1 Corinthians 13:4) and so, kindness is expressed in real relationships that can sometimes be frustrating, challenging, and demanding. When others let us down or treat us poorly how do we respond? A harsh or dismissive remark can seem to come quickly and without a second thought. Paul encourages believers that the Spirit of God himself is at work in us to produce the fruit that pleases God and lasts to eternity. At the same time, he encourages Christians to bear the family likeness and respond to others, with the same compassion, kindness, and forgiveness that we have experienced from the Lord who 'loved us and gave himself for us' (Galatians 2:20). Jesus is not only an example of kindness but, united to him through faith, we receive the Spirit who powerfully works in us (Galatians 3:2, 5).

Before I became a Christian, I had two friends who were kind to me in ways that I did not even recognise at the time. One prayed for my conversion, and asked his friends to do the same; and another asked if I would be interested in reading John's Gospel. How grateful I am for their kindness in caring enough to offer to someone who neither desired not deserved it, 'the immeasurable riches of God's grace, expressed in his kindness to us in Christ Jesus'!

QUESTIONS FOR REFLECTION
1. Take two minutes to write a list of the ways in which you have experienced the kindness of God. Give thanks for them.
2. Why does it take the power of the Holy Spirit to produce kindness in us?
3. Ask God to show you how to be kind in some difficult situation you are facing.

PRAYER
Loving heavenly Father,
in your kindness you have made known the riches of
your grace in Jesus;
teach us to love our enemies and forgive as we have
been forgiven,
that we may be clothed with Christ,
who lives and reigns with you and the Holy Spirit
one God, forever and ever. *Amen.*

Kanishka Raffel is the Dean of St. Andrew's Cathedral in Sydney, Australia.

15. Goodness

Bible Reading
Luke 6:43-45

No good tree bears bad fruit, nor does a bad tree bear good fruit. Each tree is recognised by its own fruit. People do not pick figs from thornbushes, or grapes from briers. A good man brings good things out of the good stored up in his heart, and an evil man brings evil things out of the evil stored up in his heart. For the mouth speaks what the heart is full of.

Starter Question
What do the words you've spoken in the past day or week reveal about what's in your heart?

Today's Text
But the fruit of the Spirit is love, joy, peace, forbearance,
kindness, goodness, faithfulness, gentleness and self-
control. Against such things there is no law.
Galatians 5:22-23

At funerals, people often say that the deceased was a good
person. What do we base that on? Maybe they were a loving parent who worked hard for their family. They were
compassionate, loyal, always willing to help others; honest and
humble. These are admirable qualities. But what does 'goodness'
mean according to the Bible?

In Galatians 6, Paul expands on this theme, saying 'Let us not
become weary in doing good, for at the proper time we will reap
a harvest if we do not give up. Therefore, as we have opportunity,
let us do good to all people, especially to those who belong to the
family of believers' (Galatians 6:9-10).

What is Goodness?
a. Goodness is practical.
Goodness requires action. We are told to 'do good' at every opportunity. Paul doesn't let us off the hook by making goodness a
personality trait, or something we practice occasionally. Rather,
goodness is a consistent decision to serve others at our own expense. It can be costly, as Paul suggests it can weary us if we don't
have the right perspective.

b. Goodness is objective.
Surely our definition of goodness cannot be subjective. This world
calls many things good that aren't good at all. We must look to
God to know what is good—whatever pleases him, reflects his
character, and displays his goodness to others.

c. Goodness is indiscriminate.

We can't be content with doing good to our family and close friends. Or distant, needy people who we send a cheque to without personal engagement. No, we must do good to all, but especially to our brothers and sisters in Christ. Once you've been involved in a church for a while, you realise how hard it can be to offer consistent, self-sacrificial good works. But that is what we are called to.

The Root of Goodness

Even though goodness is practical, it's not merely an action. It's not an outward act we can put on to impress others—or worse, to impress God. We can't fake it for long.

Our reading from Luke 6 says that words and actions come from our heart. We live in line with who we are. And our lack of real goodness is obvious every day—in our selfish decisions, our willing blindness to injustice, our harsh words and thoughts.

The Fruit of Goodness

So we need help. Relying on ourselves is a dead end because we can't change our own hearts. The whole point of Galatians is that salvation is by faith not works. Self-made goodness cannot save us.

Instead, we must rely on God to change our heart. That's precisely why Paul lists goodness among the fruit of the Spirit. When the Spirit dwells in our hearts, we'll produce the fruit of goodness in our lives—as the Bible repeatedly commands us to do (e.g. Ephesians 2:10, Titus 3:8, 1 Timothy 6:18).

God's Goodness

How does the indwelling Spirit change us? He is the Spirit of truth (John 16:13) who helps us to accept the truth about God and what he has done for us. Through his enabling we see the steadfast, everlasting goodness of God (Psalm 100:5, Psalm 86:5, Nehemiah 9:20, Lamentations 3:25, and more). God is not just the prime example of what is good, he *defines* good.

Our goodness springs from knowing more and more of God's goodness towards us. What better example could we have than what we celebrate at Easter? Jesus taught us to love our enemies as well as our friends (Luke 6:27). Then he lived that out: 'But God demonstrates his own love for us in this: While we were still sinners, Christ died for us' (Romans 5:8). This demonstration of goodness drives us forward, by the Spirit, to do good to others. He captivates us with thankfulness for what Jesus has done and forms us into his image.

So when we see a beggar on the street, the Spirit moves us to compassion by reminding us that we are beggars before Christ. When our family leaves dishes piled up in the sink again, we wash them without complaint because Jesus humbled himself to serve us. When we're tempted to snap at somebody who has annoyed us, we think of Jesus's gentle forbearance and hold our tongue.

All through the Spirit's work in our hearts, not our own efforts.

QUESTIONS FOR REFLECTION
1. How has God been good to you? Does this motivate you to do good to others?
2. What generally keeps you from doing good—is it busyness, self-centredness, apathy? Bring those excuses before God and ask him to change your heart.
3. Think of at least one person from each sphere of your life: family, friends, co-workers, church, neighbours, the wider country or world. What specific actions can you take this week to point these people to Jesus by doing good to them?

PRAYER

Almighty and perfect God,
who alone is good and worthy of all praise:
flood our hearts with thankfulness for what you have
done for us in your Son,
helping us to love and do good to all we meet,
especially other believers,
that we may display your goodness throughout the
whole world,
and that many might come to trust in
Jesus Christ our Saviour,
in whose name we pray,
Amen.

Cassie Watson *is a ministry apprentice at Merrylands Anglican Church in Sydney, Australia and a blogger for the Gospel Coalition Australia.*

16. Faithfulness

Bible Reading
1 Corinthians 1:4-9

I always thank my God for you because of his grace given you in Christ Jesus. For in him you have been enriched in every way—with all kinds of speech and with all knowledge—God thus confirming our testimony about Christ among you. Therefore you do not lack any spiritual gift as you eagerly wait for our Lord Jesus Christ to be revealed. He will also keep you firm to the end, so that you will be blameless on the day of our Lord Jesus Christ. God is faithful, who has called you into fellowship with his Son, Jesus Christ our Lord.

Starter Question
What does faithfulness mean for you?

TODAY'S TEXT
But the fruit of the Spirit is love, joy, peace, forbearance,
kindness, goodness, faithfulness, gentleness and self-
control. Against such things there is no law.
Galatians 5:22-23

In 1979 the historian and social critic, Christopher Lasch
wrote in *The Culture of Narcissism*: 'Our society has made lasting friendships, love affairs and marriages, increasingly difficult to achieve. Social life has become more and more warlike and
personal relationships have taken on the character of combat...'

Even though Lasch was writing 40 years ago, his thesis is still
relevant. Driven by changing and conflicting worldviews, society today has become more and more divided. For centuries, the
Judaeo-Christian worldview formed the social bond in the West.
Now we are adrift on the ocean of life without an agreed moral
compass. In *God is Good for You*, Dr Greg Sheriden writes: 'The
primary challenge today is not intellectual but cultural...'

The nine facets of the fruit of the Spirit that Paul identifies
in Galatians 5:22-23 challenge us. While all the facets are tightly
interconnected as aspects of the one fruit, it is helpful to reflect on
each. In this chapter we consider faithfulness, that translates the
literal word, faith.

FAITH AND FAITHFULNESS
Faith is a rich word that lies at the heart of the New Testament—
and not least in the letters of Paul the Apostle. For Paul, and the
rest of the New Testament, we appropriate the fulness of God's
blessing of salvation through faith in Jesus Christ. Men and wom-
en can only stand righteous or justified before God on the basis of
their faith in God's work of grace.

In Romans 3:21-22 we read: 'But now apart from the law the
righteousness of God has been made known, to which the Law and
the Prophets testify. This righteousness is given through faith in Je-

sus Christ to all who believe.' Earlier in the chapter, Paul has stressed the faithfulness of God in keeping his promises over against the faithlessness of God's ancient people, Israel (Romans 3:3).

Furthermore, faith is not simply the belief that God exists. Rather, it involves a personal and vital relationship with God through the Lord Jesus Christ. And it begins when we turn to God (repent) and put our trust (faith) in God's good news (gospel). This faith is in the God whose nature is one of love and justice, goodness and compassion—as, for example, we read in 1 John 1:9, 'If we confess our sins, he is faithful and just and will forgive us our sins and purify us from all unrighteousness.'

That said, faith is not just a matter of intellectual assent. It involves a new way of living, a new heart that directs our thinking, our choices, and our actions. It means so walking through life that we long to be faithful to the One who in his extraordinary love for us and commitment to us is absolutely faithful. Jesus says: 'I am the good shepherd; I know my sheep and my sheep know me—just as the Father knows me and I know the Father' (John 10:14-15).

God's faithfulness and ours

It is because God is faithful, because he can be trusted, that his people are also called to be faithful and dependable. We need God's word to teach us what this means and his Spirit to enable us to live it out—keeping our word and honouring our promises, not least in marriage. Another example of faithfulness is found in Luke 16:10 where we read: 'Whoever can be trusted with very little can also be trusted with much'. God's people are to be reliable stewards of the resources God gives us—especially money.

Faithfulness is also called for in talking about God's good news to those around us and beyond. And we all have a part to play in this. Not many are called to be up-front evangelists, but we can all pray for people we long to see come to Christ. We can all invite a friend to gospel conversations and church.

We are all called to be steadfast, remaining firm in our faith in Christ no matter the pressures of the voices around us. God is faithful. Jesus tells us: 'I will build my church, and the gates of Hades will not overcome it' (Matthew 16:18).

As I write, drenching rain has broken a long, devastating drought on the Australian east coast. When a media outlet headline said, 'An Answer to Prayer', the response from a minority was swift and vitriolic: 'How dare you...!' A symptom of our changing world that espouses tolerance but only if we adopt the values of the new morality. In the midst of the challenges we need to pray that we will be found faithful.

Questions for Reflection
1. What do you know of God's faithfulness in your own life?
2. Take a few minutes to consider what faithfulness in your walk with God looks like.
3. Why is faithfulness often lacking in the life of professing Christians?

Prayer
Merciful God,
by whose gift alone your faithful people
offer you true and pleasing service:
grant that we may so faithfully serve you in this life
that we do not fail at the end to obtain
your heavenly promises;
through the merits of Jesus Christ our Lord, *Amen.*

John G. Mason is President of the Anglican Connection, Commissary to the Archbishop of Sydney in the USA, and was the Founding Minister of Christ Church New York City and what is now Emmanuel Anglican Church NYC.

17. GENTLENESS

BIBLE READING
Matthew 11:28-30

Jesus said: 'Come to me, all you who are weary and burdened, and I will give you rest. Take my yoke upon you and learn from me, for I am gentle and humble in heart, and you will find rest for your souls. For my yoke is easy and my burden is light.'

STARTER QUESTION
When was the last time you observed someone acting in a gentle manner? What did they do that struck you as gentle?

Today's Text

But the fruit of the Spirit is love, joy, peace, forbearance,
kindness, goodness, faithfulness, gentleness and self-
control. Against such things there is no law.

Galatians 5:22-23

Recently, my 2-year-old nephew met his 6-week-old cousin
for the first time. He spent the entire afternoon trying to
'share' all his toys with the baby, which entailed delight-
edly shoving each toy in his cousin's little face so he might best
appreciate each and every one. I, on the other hand, spent the
entire afternoon repeatedly calling out, 'Matthew, you need to be
gentle with the baby. Be gentle!' It was at that point that I realised
our tendency to link gentleness with being 'like a little child' is
perhaps somewhat misplaced!

Galatians 5:22-23 calls Christians to bear the spiritual fruit of
gentleness. Yet how ought we to think about gentleness? How do
we understand it? What does it look like in action?

Jesus and Gentleness's Content

If we truly wish to know what gentleness is, then surely we should
look no further than the one who declares, 'I am gentle' (Matthew
11:29). That passage is a very familiar one to many of us (even appearing in the *Book of Common Prayer* Communion service). And
yet, when we look more closely, I think we find something perhaps
a little unexpected about this concept of gentleness.

We tend to define gentleness as characterising the way we are
called to act, and interact, in this world. For us, gentleness is so
often a matter of conduct. However, in this Gospel passage, Jesus doesn't simply describe himself as someone who acts gently.
Rather, he says 'I am gentle.' Jesus's gentleness is more than mere
conduct, more than simply his manner. Rather, his gentleness has
a nature. It has content. Jesus acts gently, because he is gentle.

In that same verse, the content of Jesus's gentleness is closely linked with his humility. In fact, the connection between gentleness and humility is a frequent refrain throughout the rest of the New Testament (e.g., 2 Corinthians 10:1; Ephesians 4:2; Colossians 3:12). But it is perhaps no more wonderfully recounted than in Matthew 21:1-11, when Jesus sends his disciples to fetch a donkey that he may ride into Jerusalem. We are told that this odd request took place to fulfil the prophecy that the 'king comes to you, gentle and riding on a donkey' (see Zechariah 9:9). Surely there can be no clearer demonstration of gentleness than this? The king, entering his royal city, being praised by his people... all while knowingly riding towards his death on the back of, not a noble steed, but an ordinary donkey.

Here we see the content of Jesus's gentleness. It is his willingness to bring himself low; to temper his might with meekness; to demonstrate his strength with sacrifice; to willingly give his life as a ransom for many. Jesus teaches us that the content of gentleness is not weakness. Rather it is strength that has been sacrificially tempered by love and which is eagerly directed towards bearing the burdens of others—even the burdens of the most undeserving.

Christians and gentleness's conduct
What does this definition of gentleness's content mean for our exhortation to its conduct in Galatians 5:22-23?

If we are indeed to learn from Jesus's gentleness, then certainly we are to act gently towards all others and in all circumstances (e.g., Titus 3:2, Philippians 4:5). That is, rather than being people who assert our strength, our position, our "rights", we are urged to make ourselves low, to lovingly serve others—even when they would dismiss, or even hate us for doing so.

And yet Paul's words to the Galatians were written within a specific context. The church in that ancient city had become mired in internal division, quarrels, enmity, factions, and false teaching. Paul's distress at the way they had forsaken both the gospel, and each other, is readily apparent throughout the epistle. He urgently calls them to put such desires of the flesh to death and, instead, to bear the fruit of the Spirit.

Gentleness is part of that fruit. The apostle calls his Christian readers to put aside their internal quarrelling, their enmity, their divisions with each other. He challenges them to stop conceitedly asserting themselves at the expense of others within the church. He exhorts them to cease biting and devouring other brothers and sisters in Christ. And he urges them to be gentle towards each other. To soften strength with sacrifice. To mitigate might with meekness. To not build themselves up in self-righteousness, but to 'serve one another humbly in love' (Galatians 5:13).

Gentleness is not weak or insipid. It is love's strength in humble, burden-bearing and sacrificial action. And Jesus people are called to bear it in our life together.

QUESTIONS FOR REFLECTION

1. Why does Jesus speak of his gentleness alongside his call for weary and burdened souls to come to him for rest?
2. What would be the marks of a church congregation that intentionally sought to treat each other with gentleness? What is the relationship between such gentleness, accountability for godly living, and commitment to maintaining biblical truth?
3. How might cultivating the spiritual fruit of gentleness impact the way Christians respond to the 'culture of outrage' that seems so prevalent today?

PRAYER

Gracious God,
in your Son is found true might in loving meekness,
true strength in servant-hearted sacrifice:
help us to indeed learn from Jesus,
so that we might better understand and testify
to the gentle graciousness you have shown us in him.
We pray this through the one who brings
rest to our souls,
Jesus Christ our Lord,
Amen.

Dani Treweek *is a deacon within the Anglican Diocese of Sydney and the chair of the Single Minded Conference.*

18. SELF-CONTROL

BIBLE READING
Proverbs 25:28
Like a city whose walls are broken through
is a person who lacks self-control.

STARTER QUESTION
When did you last give thought to how self-controlled you are?

Today's Text
But the fruit of the Spirit is love, joy, peace, forbearance,
kindness, goodness, faithfulness, gentleness and self-
control. Against such things there is no law.
Galatians 5:22-23

Self-control is last in Paul's list in Galatians 5:22-23. This
does not mean that it is less important than other aspects
of the fruit of the Spirit. We will consider four questions on
self-control: What is it? How do we become self-controlled? How
important is self-control in our lives as Christians? And in what
kind of situations do we need to exercise self-control?

WHAT IS SELF-CONTROL?
There is something that threatens to get out of control. It needs to
be restrained. If it is not restrained it will have devastating consequences. The thing we are talking about here is the self, with all its
desires and ambitions. Self-control goes beyond external exercises
or practises. It deals with the inner desires of the self that are opposed to the way of the Spirit. In Galatians 5:19-21, just before he
talks about the fruit of the Spirit, Paul lists the works of the flesh.
Among them is selfish ambition.

The self wants its own things, at its own time, with no regard
to God and his people—and at times with no regard to its own
resulting destruction. Left to its own devices, the self will go the
way of the flesh. An example of this is when King David did not
exercise self-control, but yielded to his lust after seeing Bathsheba
bathing (2 Samuel 11).

Self-control is the ability to restrain or master oneself. In my
isiXhosa language, the term is 'ukuzeyisa.' It carries with it the notion of defeating your own self. In the face of a desire, a temptation,
or an opportunity to do wrong before the Lord, self-control is the
ability to say no and stop yourself from following your evil desires.
It is the courage to act in opposition to the demands of the flesh.

How do we become self-controlled?

Galatians 5:22-23 show us that self-control in the life of a believer is the fruit of the Spirit. This means that self-control is not something we can have by our own will power alone. There is no set of laws to be followed or routines to be practised in order for the children of God to possess self-control.

Rather, it is the result of the Holy Spirit indwelling us. A fruit tree that has life in it will produce fruit of its kind. In the same way, the Spirit who lives in us to give us life produces his fruit in us. The fruit becomes evident externally. However, it is something that has been growing internally for a period of time. Because the Spirit lives among Christians, it is inevitable that in due time the fruit of the Spirit will be evident in the Christian's life. You cannot be indwelled by the Spirit of God and not have the fruit of the Spirit growing gradually in you.

This does not take away our responsibility to pray to God to graciously bring about self-control in us. By the power of the Holy Spirit, we need to walk in step with the Spirit. Did not Christ exercise self-control when he resisted the devil during his 40 day fast in the wilderness? As we study and meditate on the sufficiency of Christ in our life, we will find ourselves content and joyful to exercise self-control.

How important is self-control?

Can a Christian be happy with lack of self-control in their own life? The answer is no. You see, if self-control is the fruit of the Spirit, then not to possess it in increasing measure should be a cause for concern. Christians prove themselves to be Christians not by their gifts but by the fruit of the Spirit emanating from them. The godly character traits in the believer should be plain for all to see. The fruit of the Spirit, of which self-control is a part, is a sign that one is abiding in Jesus Christ who is the true vine. Self-control is among the qualifications required of a Christian leader in 1 Timothy 3 and in Titus 2. Without self-control a person would be out of control. They would please the desires of the flesh that lust against the Spirit.

When should we exercise self-control?

None of us is perfect. We are a work in progress. God is not finished with us. We have sometimes used these statements to avoid exercising self-control in certain areas of our life. Self-control is supposed to be practised in every area of a Christian's life. Whenever we are tempted and we desire to think or act out of our selfish desires, we must ask God to grant us grace to exercise self-control. This kind of self-control brings glory to God.

Questions for Reflection

1. How has this chapter helped you understand self-control in biblical terms?
2. How has self-control grown in you over the last few years?
3. In which areas of your life are you praying that the Lord may help you to exercise this fruit of the Spirit?

Prayer

Gracious Father,
you have given us your Spirit to dwell within us:
grant us growth in self-control,
in order to resist lusts of the flesh
which war against you,
and to walk in the Spirit,
through your Son and our Saviour Jesus Christ,
Amen.

Phumezo Masango serves as Rector of Christ Church Khayelitsha, and teaches at George Whitefield College in Cape Town, South Africa.

the
SEVEN
DEADLY
SINS

19. PRIDE

BIBLE READING
3 John

The elder,

To my dear friend Gaius, whom I love in the truth.

Dear friend, I pray that you may enjoy good health and that all may go well with you, even as your soul is getting along well. It gave me great joy when some believers came and testified about your faithfulness to the truth, telling how you continue to walk in it. I have no greater joy than to hear that my children are walking in the truth.

Dear friend, you are faithful in what you are doing for the brothers and sisters, even though they are strangers to you. They have told the church about your love. Please send them on their way in a manner that honours God. It was for the sake of the Name that they went out, receiving no help from the pagans. We ought therefore to show hospitality to such people so that we may work together for the truth.

I wrote to the church, but Diotrephes, who loves to be first, will not welcome us. So when I come, I will call attention to what he is doing, spreading malicious nonsense about us. Not satisfied with that, he even refuses to welcome other believers. He also stops those who want to do so and puts them out of the church.

Dear friend, do not imitate what is evil but what is good. Anyone who does what is good is from God. Anyone who does what is evil has not seen God. Demetrius is well spoken of by everyone—and even by the truth itself. We also speak well of him, and you know that our testimony is true.

I have much to write to you, but I do not want to do so with pen and ink. I hope to see you soon, and we will talk face to face.

Peace to you. The friends here send their greetings. Greet the friends there by name.

STARTER QUESTION
What would persuade you that the person you're talking to is a proud individual?

Today's Text
To fear the LORD is to hate evil; I hate pride and
arrogance, evil behaviour and perverse speech.
Proverbs 8:13

Sin is deadly. It's not a cuddly toy that should be squeezed for comfort. Rather, it's the spiritual equivalent of gangrene, progressively killing any life it finds in its path. The Bible expertly diagnoses many different types of sin, and leaves us in no doubt about the consequences of unchecked rebellion against God. Sin kills. It can lead a person to experience eternal death in hell. And it can kill our experience of joy and delight in this earthly existence.

The so-called Seven Deadly Sins are obviously not a complete list of biblical vices. However, this list is a good place to start if we are to mortify some of our most deadly spiritual diseases.

Pride
Proud people have an overestimated sense of their own importance and foolishly devalue those around them. The result is carnage in relationships.

In 3 John 11 we are told 'do not imitate what is evil but what is good.' And what is striking is that in this New Testament letter we are presented with three examples, either to copy or avoid: Gaius, Diotrephes, and Demetrius. Diotrephes is most relevant for our topic as he is a man full of pride. Only five words are required to summarise his character: he loves to be first.

Mark Twain, the American novelist, once had the unsettling experience of reading his own obituary in the New York Journal. After pulling himself together, he wrote to the editor to assure him that the report of his death was an exaggeration. If you were to die tonight, what would they write about you tomorrow? This is what they wrote about Diotrephes: he loves to be first. What a depressing summary of human existence! Imagine everything you do being driven by the agenda of self-promotion. It would be so tragic.

And yet this is how Diotrephes consumed each 24-hour window.

This pride fuelled-existence was deadly for relationships in the church. This is what we read in verse 10, "when I come, I will call attention to what he is doing, spreading malicious nonsense about us. Not satisfied with that, he even refuses to welcome other believers. He also stops those who want to do so and puts them out of the church." There is no evidence here of disagreements over doctrine. This is a personality issue. Relationship carnage fuelled by sinful pride. And the gospel impact was devastating. Gospel fellowship is destroyed. Missionaries are not welcomed. And the church is split apart.

We need to be challenged by the example of Diotrephes. He is an example of evil to be avoided at all costs.

COMBATTING PRIDE

The key question is; how can we combat a desire to be first? How can we put to death the deadly sin of pride? Here are two suggestions.

First, gaze at Jesus. Let's contemplate how wonderful Jesus is. He is full of love and compassion. He is our glorious Saviour who has given us everything we have. Our salvation and sanctification are both gifts from him. We cannot boast if we recognise the goodness of Jesus in our every triumph. We don't need to deny godly progress. Instead, we acknowledge the true source of everything good in our lives.

Second, listen to others. Our temptation when speaking to others is to promote ourselves at every opportunity. We like to speak more than we listen. And when we listen, we love to talk about our own lives in response to what people say. However, there is a different way, a better way. There is a way to strangle our pride if we decide to listen more than we speak. And when we listen, not to respond by endlessly talking about how achievements in our own life connect with what we've just heard. This won't be easy. But, by the power of the Holy Spirit, we will see breakthroughs and joyful battles won.

Pride is a relationship killer. But by God's grace, we can learn to live again.

QUESTIONS FOR REFLECTION

1. He loved to be first. How similar are you to Diotrephes?
2. How can we help each other gaze at Jesus?
3. What victories have you won against pride in the last few years?

PRAYER

Almighty God,
creator and sustainer of all life,
who gives us everything we need for our sanctification:
help us to gaze on the Lord Jesus Christ,
that we may kill our pride within,
and instead live a life of joyful humility,
through Jesus Christ, our Lord and Saviour,
Amen.

Lee McMunn *is the Senior Minister of Trinity Church Scarborough, and Planting Director of the Anglican Mission in England (AMiE)*

20. GREED

BIBLE READING
Colossians 3:5
Put to death, therefore, whatever belongs to your earthly nature: sexual immorality, impurity, lust, evil desires and greed, which is idolatry.

STARTER QUESTION
Is Paul's condemnation of greed as idolatry just exaggeration for effect?

TODAY'S TEXT

But godliness with contentment is great gain. For we
brought nothing into the world, and we can take nothing out of it. But if we have food and clothing, we will be
content with that. Those who want to get rich fall into
temptation and a trap and into many foolish and harmful desires that plunge people into ruin and destruction.
For the love of money is a root of all kinds of evil. Some
people, eager for money, have wandered from the faith
and pierced themselves with many griefs.

1 Timothy 6:6-10

I n recent years a number of academics and social commentators
have questioned the rampant materialism of the Western world.
They argue that if people are trying to get rich in order to be
happy, it isn't working. Studies show that Western happiness has
declined precisely in tandem with the rise of affluence. Apparently,
those who strive most for wealth tend to live with lower wellbeing.
What, then, drives our desire for more material possessions?

Some critics of greed have compared it to a religion. One news-
paper article carried the title, 'In greed we trust' (instead of 'in
God we trust'). A review of Robert Kiyosaki's *Rich Dad, Poor Dad*
commented that it 'isn't just a wealth creation manual, it's a religious tract.' As it turns out, the comparison of greed with a religion is hardly original. Along with Paul's condemnation of greed
as a form of idol worship in Colossians 3:5 (and Ephesians 5:5),
Jesus charged that people either serve God or Mammon (i.e., possessions; Matthew 6:24 / Luke 16:13).

THE BIBLE'S CONDEMNATION OF GREED AS A RELIGION

What are we to make of the comparison of greed to a false religion?
Can such extreme rhetoric help us in the fight against greed today?

In what ways are greed and idolatry alike? Over the centuries
three answers to this question have been suggested. Whereas most

twentieth-century interpreters see love as the point of similarity, the Reformer Martin Luther identified trust, and the Church Father Chrysostom, service. Do the greedy person and the idolater love, trust, and serve their money and their idols respectively? All three are in fact correct.

The Bible underscores love, trust, and service as three core responses of the believer in relation to God, and faults both the idolater and the greedy person for foolishly misdirecting these same three. Both idolaters and the greedy 'set their hearts' on inappropriate objects. Both 'rely on,' 'trust in', and 'look to' their 'treasures' for protection and blessing. Both 'serve' and 'submit to' things that demean rather than ennoble the worshipper. Greed is idolatry in that, like the literal worship of idols, it represents an attack on God's exclusive rights to human love, trust, and service. Material things can replace God in the human heart and set us on a course that is opposed to him, even arousing his jealousy.

THE CONTEMPORARY RELEVANCE OF GREED AS IDOLATRY

Is greed a religion today? It does seem that for many people material things hold a place in their lives that was once occupied by belief in God. The economy has achieved what might be described as a sacred status. Like God, the economy, is capable of supplying our needs without limit. Also, like God, the economy is mysterious, dangerous, and intransigent, despite the best managerial efforts of its associated clergy.

In our day, the very things Christianity claims God expects of believers, namely love, trust, and service, can easily characterise our relationship with money. A glance at the palpable glee on the faces of game show contestants confirms our love of money. You can literally buy 'securities' and 'futures.' Most disturbingly, as the French ethicist Jacques Ellul put it, 'We can use money, but it is really money that uses us and makes us servants by bringing us under its law and subordinating us to its aims.'

The ultimate solution to the insatiable grasping for, and obsessive hoarding of, material things that marks our age is not simply to say no to something of limited value, but to say yes to something better. Jesus's concluding exhortation on the subject of greed in the Sermon on the Mount amounts to such a redirection of desire: 'The pagans run after such things... But you instead should seek first God's kingdom and righteousness' (Matthew 6:32-33). The best defence against the love of money and the desire to get really rich, is to love God and long to be rich towards him.

Economists may recommend greed, politicians rely on it, and celebrities flaunt it, but in the end like all idols, money fails to deliver on its promises. If the root cause of materialism is misdirected religious impulses, then the ultimate solution is still faith in the true and living God, who alone gives the security and satisfaction that each of us craves.

Questions for Reflection

1. Are you tempted to love, trust, or serve money? Which one is a problem for you?
2. What about God and the plan of salvation might help you to be more content with your lot in life?
3. What about God and the plan of salvation might help you to be more generous in sharing your possessions?

Prayer
Immortal God,
who richly supplies us with everything for our enjoyment:
help those of us who are rich in this present world to
be generous and willing to share
and to flee the love of money,
that we may take hold of the life that is truly life,
until the glorious appearing of our Lord Jesus Christ,
in whose name we pray, *Amen.*

Brian Rosner is the Principal of Ridley College, Melbourne, Australia, and is the author of a number of books, including Greed as Idolatry *and* Beyond Greed.

21. LUST

2 Samuel 11:1-5

In the spring, at the time when kings go off to war, David sent Joab out with the king's men and the whole Israelite army. They destroyed the Ammonites and besieged Rabbah. But David remained in Jerusalem. One evening David got up from his bed and walked around on the roof of the palace. From the roof he saw a woman bathing. The woman was very beautiful, and David sent someone to find out about her. The man said, 'She is Bathsheba, the daughter of Eliam and the wife of Uriah the Hittite.' Then David sent messengers to get her. She came to him, and he slept with her. (Now she was purifying herself from her monthly uncleanness.) Then she went back home. The woman conceived and sent word to David, saying, 'I am pregnant.'

STARTER QUESTION

In what ways do our culture and the painful, personal circumstances of life nudge us towards impurity?

Today's Text
Psalm 51:1-12

For the director of music. A psalm of David.
When the prophet Nathan came to him after David had committed
adultery with Bathsheba.

Have mercy on me, O God,
    according to your unfailing love;
according to your great compassion
    blot out my transgressions.
Wash away all my iniquity
    and cleanse me from my sin.
For I know my transgressions,
    and my sin is always before me.
Against you, you only, have I sinned
    and done what is evil in your sight;
so you are right in your verdict
    and justified when you judge.
Surely I was sinful at birth,
    sinful from the time my mother conceived me.
Yet you desired faithfulness even in the womb;
    you taught me wisdom in that secret place.
Cleanse me with hyssop, and I will be clean;
    wash me, and I will be whiter than snow.
Let me hear joy and gladness;
    let the bones you have crushed rejoice.
Hide your face from my sins
    and blot out all my iniquity.
Create in me a pure heart, O God,
    and renew a steadfast spirit within me.
Do not cast me from your presence
    or take your Holy Spirit from me.
Restore to me the joy of your salvation
    and grant me a willing spirit, to sustain me.

It was a stressful time. The responsibilities were weighing heavily on his heart. No-one could share his burdens—no-one could fully understand the pressure or pain. He just wanted some release—a moment of comfort, a chance to indulge. 'And why shouldn't I?' he thought to himself, 'I deserve to have what I want.' And so, he acted. He gave in to his sordid and sinful desires. Fully aware his actions were wrong. Far from ignorant of what the consequences could be. In the moment, he didn't care about godliness, respect, dignity, or love—lust won the day and what he saw, and wanted, he took.

It's the story of a King reigning a thousand years before Christ—adulterous, abusive, reckless with the responsibility of his role. It's the tale of a businessman in a 21st century town, logging on to porn at the end of another frustrating day. It's the narrative of a woman, sitting alone, running headlong into a fantasy that pretends to offer the intimacy she so desperately desires. The reality of many a Christian—male, female, young, old—whose glance lingers a little too long, whose imagination plunges into depths so dark, whose text messages flirt with leading others astray. We know it's not right. We proclaim that purity is best. But somehow, some days, our sexual drives win and we hate ourselves for our rebellious ways.

HIDING IN THE DARK
Of all the sins with which we can struggle, lust is the one we keep most firmly in the dark. If people knew the content of our thoughts, our dreams, our actions, we imagine repulsion and rejection would be the order of the day. Our instinct is to hide, to cover, to deny. Maybe we don't go as far as King David. He, discovering Bathsheba was pregnant, tried to manufacture a sexual encounter between her and her spouse, when that failed, he opted for murder by proxy: send Uriah to the front, he'll have no chance of surviving there. But our attempts to cover our tracks are no more pleasing to God. Proudly asserting we have accountability software (when all too often we turn it off), being able to lead a Bible study on purity (when the latest smutty novel sits by our

bed), or modelling wise boundaries on a Sunday (while fantasising wildly on a Saturday night), may give the impression of godliness—but the One who matters most is not taken in.

It took a wise and brave prophet, in Nathan, to approach and rebuke David for his sin. He reminded him that when we lust after another we take what does not belong to us. We objectify, use for our own pleasure, those who are precious image-bearers and loved by the Lord. It hurts those around but, most importantly, it dishonours the One who made us and calls us to live a life honouring him. At its core, lust is a worship-disorder: we take our eyes off Christ and elevate our desire for satisfaction above his throne.

HOPE OF CLEANSING

But all is not lost. Even the most hardened sexual sinners can find forgiveness in God's grace-filled arms. When we turn to him, in true repentance and faith, the wonder that King David was able to express in Psalm 51 can be ours as well: washed whiter than snow, a renewed joy in our salvation, and a mouth full of praise. Doesn't that sound better than wallowing in the shame of hidden lust?

Of course, there may be consequences for our wayward behaviour. The legacy of David's atrocity lingered in his family for years. We may need help to overcome an addiction, a time of restoration with someone we have wounded or tossed aside, accountability for future conduct—we'll need our brothers and sisters every step of the way. But there's hope. There's a calling to a life, centred on Christ, which is increasingly pure, more fulfilling, and ever more beautiful than anything our darker desires could achieve. And, through Jesus's work on the cross, that life is no pipe-dream. Washed clean, empowered by the Spirit, and with eyes fixed on eternity, a passion for purity is a privilege we all can enjoy.

Questions for Reflection

1. Are there struggles with lust which you are currently indulging or hiding rather than addressing? What desires are you seeing as more important than Jesus and his call?
2. How can the Psalm 51 reminder of grace spur you on to a life of repentance and faith?
3. What would it look like for you to seek the help of others as you pursue purity? Or what would it look like for you to stand alongside others as they battle sexual temptation week by week?

Prayer
Holy God,
who, in accordance with your
nature and good purposes,
called us to a life of purity and trust:
mercifully grant that we, who know the futility of lust,
may turn to you for grace and hope;
through the love of the Father,
the cleansing of the Son,
and the sanctifying work of the Spirit, *Amen.*

Helen Thorne is a freelance speaker and author of Purity is Possible. She attends Dundonald Church, Wimbledon.

22. ENVY

BIBLE READING
Psalm 73:1-13
A psalm of Asaph.

Surely God is good to Israel,
>   to those who are pure in heart.
But as for me, my feet had almost slipped;
>   I had nearly lost my foothold.
For I envied the arrogant
>   when I saw the prosperity of the wicked.
They have no struggles;
>   their bodies are healthy and strong.
They are free from common human burdens;
>   they are not plagued by human ills.
Therefore pride is their necklace;
>   they clothe themselves with violence.
From their callous hearts comes iniquity;
>   their evil imaginations have no limits.
They scoff, and speak with malice;
>   with arrogance they threaten oppression.
Their mouths lay claim to heaven,
>   and their tongues take possession of the earth.
Therefore their people turn to them
>   and drink up waters in abundance.
They say, "How would God know?
>   Does the Most High know anything?"
This is what the wicked are like—
>   always free of care, they go on amassing wealth.
Surely in vain I have kept my heart pure
>   and have washed my hands in innocence.

STARTER QUESTION
How might envy be the opposite of peace?

TODAY'S TEXT
A heart at peace gives life to the body,
but envy rots the bones.
Proverbs 14:30

E nvy tends to be one of those insidious, secret sins that is far too easy not to acknowledge or even be aware of. It can be a creeping thought, a vague state of mind, a general malaise with what your home, or job, or body, or marriage looks like. It's fifteen minutes on Facebook, putting your phone down with a grimace of dissatisfaction you might not even realise you've made. And yet what is the result? It rots your bones.

THE DESTRUCTIVENESS OF ENVY
That is because as ephemeral as envy may seem, it is utterly destructive. As James admonishes in his letter, 'where you have envy and selfish ambition, there you find disorder and every evil practice' (James 3:16). Envy might start as a simple question. Why don't I have… why can't I be like… Yet that seemingly innocent question has, at its root, a lack of faith, not just in God's provision, but his entire character.

Envy often starts out small. A dictionary definition is 'a feeling of discontented or resentful longing aroused by someone else's possessions, qualities, or luck.' Someone at work gets a promotion. A neighbour's house is bigger than yours. Or maybe it's not about material possessions, which can make envy even more insidious and harder to recognise—your friend's children seem to have it more together. Your colleague's ministry is so much more fruitful. Yet instead of being encouraged or perhaps necessarily convicted by their blessing, you feel bitterness that you are not having the same experience. Resentful longing takes root. And from that terrible little seed, a terrible, destructive vine grows and twines around your heart, choking everything.

Envy becomes destructive when we feed it, which we, in our

sinful state, like to do. We have an unfortunate tendency to luxuriate in the self-righteous, self-pitying reflections on how unfair life is. Instead of trying to 'take captive every thought to make it obedient to Christ' (2 Corinthians 10:5), we allow and even encourage those negative thoughts to fester and breed so they take over not just our minds, but our lives. We choose to view the world through a murky lens of dissatisfaction as our resentment turns into a sense of self-entitlement, anger, or even acts of violence. Saul's envy of David led to his alienation from God. David's envy of Uriah led to death. And while we might not experience such dramatically dreadful results in our own lives, envy can still be just as harmful in its small and insidious ways, because it causes us to doubt God's goodness, just as Adam and Eve did in the garden.

When we doubt God's goodness, we are questioning who he is. We are doubting the words of Psalm 18: 'As for God, his way is perfect: The LORD's word is flawless.' We put ourselves in God's place and we begin to believe that we know better than he does what we need and how our lives should look. So we start to think and speak and act accordingly, until we have wandered so far away from the truth we can no longer see it reflected in our lives, or even recognise it for what it is—and often we don't even realise we've moved from the solid ground we took for granted.

THE ANTIDOTE TO ENVY

So how do we battle envy? For while there is no sin in being tempted, we need to respond to that temptation rightly. The way to battle any temptation is with truth. As Peter writes, 'Therefore, rid yourselves of all malice and all deceit, hypocrisy, envy, and slander of every kind. Like newborn babies, crave pure spiritual milk, so that by it you may grow up in your salvation' (1 Peter 2:1-2).

When you spend an hour on social media and feel that twitch of resentful longing, run to the word. When you start to ask that needling question 'why don't I…?', think of something you are thankful for instead. Constantly and consistently remind yourself of God's great promises, of all he has given to us in Christ, so that you 'may know the hope to which he has called you, the riches of his glorious inheritance in his holy people, and his incomparably great power for us who believe' (Ephesians 1:18-19).

When we continually remind ourselves of the love God has lavished on us through Jesus, and that which he continues to show us in his day-to-day provision, the bigger house, the thinner body, or the better-paying job are all put in their proper perspective. As sinful creatures, we need to be reminding and reorienting ourselves day by day, sometimes minute by minute. The more truth we imbibe and imbue in our lives, the more we will be able to recognise envy for what it is—insidious and destructive.

But what if you're not envious of your neighbour's car, but their prayer life or ministry or sense of joy? This can be much harder to recognise, with its seemingly holy trappings. Sometimes seeing someone else's spiritual riches can lead to self-pity rather than conviction, repentance, and encouragement. We feel God has shortchanged us. Again, we need to run to the word. God has already given us every spiritual blessing in Christ. Let that first twinge of temptation bring a renewed desire to serve and love the Lord, the Father of heavenly lights, from whom every good and perfect gift comes.

QUESTIONS FOR REFLECTION

1. How might envy lead to further sin and destruction in your life?
2. Is there a particular area in your life where you struggle with envy? Will you repent today of this and draw near to God?
3. What aspects of God's character can you reflect on to remind you that he has given you all that you need?

PRAYER
Loving heavenly Father, our creator and sustainer,
who gives us all good things richly to enjoy:
grant us grace so to value all the blessings you lavish
upon us in Christ,
that we may neither envy nor covet the gifts of others,
but find all our contentment in him,
in whose precious name we pray,
Amen.

Katharine Swartz is an author of contemporary fiction under the name Kate Hewitt. She lives in Monmouth, Wales where her husband is chaplain to the Haberdasher schools there.

23. GLUTTONY

Proverbs 25:16
If you find honey, eat just enough—
too much of it, and you will vomit.

STARTER QUESTION
Can you have too much of a good thing?

Today's Text

Listen, my son, and be wise,
and set your heart on the right path:
Do not join those who drink too much wine
or gorge themselves on meat,
for drunkards and gluttons become poor,
and drowsiness clothes them in rags.

Proverbs 23:19-21

For most of us, the word 'gluttony' probably brings to mind a picture of someone working their way through a dozen pizzas, several packs of doughnuts, and multiple fizzy drinks. It's a reassuring picture, because few of us are quite that bad. 'Thank you, Lord, that I'm not like that', we say, all the while uneasily wondering where we've heard that prayer before (see Luke 18:11).

Food is great. It's a wonderful gift of God, to be enjoyed and used in his service. It can be used as the basis of hospitality, to minister to others. It can be used in a feast, to celebrate achievements and blessings and anniversaries. And it keeps us alive, all the while reminding us of our dependency on the God who gives all we need.

But you can have too much of a good thing—and, if we are honest, most of us do. Maybe occasionally, perhaps regularly, we don't stop when we should. Seconds? Yes, please, and thirds too, if you don't mind. One biscuit or two? Well, there are only half-a-dozen left in the packet!

Five ways to be a glutton

Before we get too comfortable, let's reflect on how the theologian Thomas Aquinas identified five ways to commit gluttony. He said:

'Now two things are to be considered in eating, namely the food we eat, and the eating of it. Accordingly, the inordinate desire may be considered in two ways. First, with regard to the food consumed: and thus, as regards

the substance or species of food a person seeks "sumptuous" i.e. costly food; as regards its quality, they seek food prepared too nicely—i.e. "daintily"; and as regards quantity, they exceed by eating "too much." Secondly, the inordinate desire is considered as to the consumption of food: either because one forestalls the proper time for eating, which is to eat "hastily," or one fails to observe the due manner of eating, by eating "greedily."'
Summa Theologiae, Part 2-2, Question 148

In other words, gluttony isn't just about eating too much. It can also be about eating food that is too luxurious or costly, or food that's too dainty or elaborate. And you can also commit gluttony by eating too hastily or too greedily. Perhaps gluttony is a bigger problem than we thought.

QUESTIONING CONSUMPTION

What does it say about the state of our hearts, when we consume far more than we need? If someone laid out all that you had consumed (food and drink) in the past week, what would it say about your self-control, your generosity of spirit, and your wisdom? And thinking about other forms of consumption, especially our spending, what do they reveal about our priorities and our pleasures? To put it bluntly: how can we be modelling godly self-control and contentment, when our actions seem to speak so much louder than any words?

Even the secular world is (quite rightly) kicking back against our society's conspicuous consumption, and asking questions about the responsible use of resources. How much more, though, should the church of Christ be questioning the attitudes of our hearts that lead to the over-indulgence and over-consumption of our age? What is it that drives us to spend so much on cars, clothing, devices, holidays, restaurants and the rest? Meanwhile, the hungry and the homeless watch and weep.

Feed on him in your hearts

There is another way. 'Listen, my son, and be wise, and set your heart on the right path: Do not join those who drink too much wine or gorge themselves on meat, for drunkards and gluttons become poor, and drowsiness clothes them in rags.' (Proverbs 23:19-21). While gluttony is bad for the glutton, and dangerous for those around them, directing our hearts in the way revealed by the Scriptures points us in a better direction.

We need to direct our hearts towards Christ. When our hearts are delighting in Christ, they are less likely to want to be distracted by conspicuous consumption. When our hearts are satisfied in Christ, we will find it easier to grow in the grace of self-control and contentment. When our hearts are rejoicing in Christ, then gluttony will be seen for the foolish disgrace that it is, and our lives will better reflect the glory of our Lord.

Questions for Reflection

1. When is gluttony a particular danger for you?
2. Why is the life of restraint more blessed than the life of gluttony?
3. What does it mean for you to 'direct your heart' in the way that helps you to be satisfied in the Lord Jesus Christ?

Prayer

Father of all goodness,
we thank you for your generous provision
of so much blessing in our lives:
give us grace to enjoy your gifts wisely;
grant us wisdom to control our appetites carefully;
and direct our hearts to delight in your ways eternally,
through Jesus Christ our Lord,
Amen.

Mark Wallace *is the Priest-in-charge of St. Peter's, Colchester and Senior Chaplain to the Bishop of Maidstone.*

24. WRATH

BIBLE READING
Romans 12:17-21

Do not repay anyone evil for evil. Be careful to do what is right in the eyes of everyone. If it is possible, as far as it depends on you, live at peace with everyone. Do not take revenge, my dear friends, but leave room for God's wrath, for it is written: 'It is mine to avenge; I will repay,' says the Lord. On the contrary:
    'If your enemy is hungry, feed him;
        if he is thirsty, give him something to drink.
    In doing this, you will heap burning coals on his head.'
Do not be overcome by evil, but overcome evil with good.

STARTER QUESTION
What has made you angry in the past two weeks?

Today's Text

But the wisdom that comes from heaven is first of all
pure; then peace-loving, considerate, submissive, full of
mercy and good fruit, impartial and sincere. Peacemakers who sow in peace reap a harvest of righteousness.
What causes fights and quarrels among you? Don't they
come from your desires that battle within you? You
desire but do not have, so you kill. You covet but you
cannot get what you want, so you quarrel and fight.
You do not have because you do not ask God. When
you ask, you do not receive, because you ask with
wrong motives, that you may spend what you get on
your pleasures.
James 3:17-4:3

All sin is ugly, but some sins seem uglier than others. Surely wrath is one of the ugliest. The word conjures up images of red-faced rage, of fist-clenched fury, of an out-of-control offensive to crush and destroy. And when described that way, most of us can put this ugly sin far from us. We're happy to condemn wrath as an ugly sin, we're also happy to thank God that we're not like 'other people' (Luke 18:11) who are afflicted with it.

And yet, the sin of wrath may be closer to us than we imagine. Wrath lives in the same semantic world as anger, and anger is compli-cated. The Bible instructs us to rid ourselves of anger (Ephesians 4:31, Colossians 3:8), assumes that we will be angry (Ephesians 4:26, James 1:19), and is happy to recount the Lord Jesus's anger (Mark 3:5).

Anger is complicated because it's good and appropriate to be angry against sin. To hear of the vulnerable being abused and tak-en advantage of, or of Christian brothers and sisters persecuted or oppressed because of their faith—these things should stir in us a response of 'that's not right!' Anger directed towards sin is good and appropriate. God's people are themselves condemned by the Lord when they are indifferent toward such evil (Amos 6:6).

WHAT MAKES YOU ANGRY?

However all too often our response of 'that's not right!' is directed towards people or circumstances which stop us getting what we want. Sin may (or may not) be present, but what really creates our anger is our little world not being the way we want it to be. At this point it isn't wrong being done against God's world and God's ways which is making us angry, but more that our rule over our little worlds and our little ways is being challenged and changed by outside forces. And so we get angry. Consider what has made you angry in recent weeks. Might there be an element of this present?

It is in this seed-bed of anger at wrong done to us that wrath slowly grows. Wrath wants more than simply restoration of our worlds to the way we want them. Wrath wants reparations to be paid and revenge to be taken. Wrath is anger with its boots on, acting to ensure that our rule over our lives is enforced and all challengers are put in their place. Wrath may run hot in the verbal outburst to the offender's face, or run cold in the subtle manipulation and slander behind their backs. It may lash out in a moment, or quietly fester for many months. But the outcome is the same. They must pay for what they have done. And we will act to ensure that they do.

WRATH AND REVENGE

And yet as Christians we are not rulers of our own lives. Jesus is Lord. And just as he entrusted himself to the one who judges justly (1 Peter 2:22), so too we are called to follow his example. This is not to say that wrong done to us doesn't matter—it most certainly does! You are a creation of God himself, made in his image and likeness. You are a child of God himself, purchased by the blood of his own Son. Wrong done to you most certainly matters, and must be—and will be—paid for.

But it is not up to us to take revenge, as though we were in sole charge of our own lives. If it were up to us our justice would likely be unjust, for we do not see the whole picture. If it were up to us our judgment would likely be hypocritical, for we are as guilty as those who have done wrong against us. Rather, as we entrust ourselves to God and his just judgement we leave room for his wrath (Romans 12:19). He will make all things right. But in doing so we also leave room for his patient grace, that those who have wronged us might flee to the one they have most grossly wronged, and seek his forgiveness. That the wrong they have done to us might be borne by the one who has done no wrong at all. And that they, like us, who were by nature deserving of wrath, might receive not justice, but the mercy of God in Christ Jesus.

QUESTIONS FOR REFLECTION

1. What makes you most angry? Is it caused by God's world and God's ways being wronged, or your world and your ways?
2. How does wrath show itself in your life? Does it run hot or cold? Fast or slow?
3. How might God's judgment, poured out on Jesus, free you to entrust to him the judgment of those who have wronged you?

PRAYER
Sovereign and saving God,
who sees clearly the thoughts and attitudes
of all hearts:
forgive our unjust anger and wrath,
and equip us to entrust all judgement to you,
that we might follow our Lord's example,
and leave room for your justice and mercy,
through Jesus Christ our Lord,
Amen.

Dave Clancey *is Vicar of Trinity South Christchurch and Chairman of the Latimer Fellowship of New Zealand.*

25. SLOTH

BIBLE READING
Proverbs 26:13-15

A sluggard says, 'There's a lion in the road,
    a fierce lion roaming the streets!'
As a door turns on its hinges,
    so a sluggard turns on his bed.
A sluggard buries his hand in the dish;
    he is too lazy to bring it back to his mouth.
A sluggard is wiser in his own eyes
    than seven people who answer discreetly.

STARTER QUESTION
Is being slothful really all that bad?

Today's Text

I do not understand what I do. For what I want to do I do not do, but what I hate I do. And if I do what I do not want to do, I agree that the law is good. As it is, it is no longer I myself who do it, but it is sin living in me. For I know that good itself does not dwell in me, that is, in my sinful nature. For I have the desire to do what is good, but I cannot carry it out. For I do not do the good I want to do, but the evil I do not want to do—this I keep on doing. Now if I do what I do not want to do, it is no longer I who do it, but it is sin living in me that does it.

So I find this law at work: Although I want to do good, evil is right there with me. For in my inner being I delight in God's law; but I see another law at work in me, waging war against the law of my mind and making me a prisoner of the law of sin at work within me. What a wretched man I am! Who will rescue me from this body that is subject to death? Thanks be to God, who delivers me through Jesus Christ our Lord!

So then, I myself in my mind am a slave to God's law, but in my sinful nature a slave to the law of sin.

Romans 7:15-25

If you've ever had occasion to stay in a hotel you'll be familiar with the 'do not disturb' signs provided for weary travellers to hang on the outside of the bedroom door to ensure the housekeeping team don't burst in with vacuum cleaners while the occupant is attempting to slumber. One such example frames the request very politely indeed: 'Please don't wake me. I want to sleep a little longer.'

Perhaps that's the image you conjure up when you hear the word 'sloth'. Of all the deadly sins we are being challenged about in this book, sloth is the one most of us know least about. Sloth is usually reduced to the idea of laziness and what, really, is so deadly about being a bit lazy? Laziness isn't really seen as much of a problem these days. It might be a minor character flaw, but is it any more serious than that? Can sloth really be called a sin—and a deadly sin at that?

The Church Fathers certainly thought so. And, whilst they might not have used the language of Seven Deadly Sins, Luther and Calvin thought so too. So what is it?

WHAT IS SLOTH?

Sloth is a stubborn and ongoing feeling of listlessness, restlessness, or boredom. It seeps into the soul and poisons the mind so that instead of revelling and delighting in the work and relationships that God has given us, and loving him with all our heart, soul, mind, and strength and our neighbour as ourselves, we seek refuge in escape, disengagement, and over-stimulation. The results are destructive.

Sloth isn't the passing experience of boredom or distraction we all know. Nor is it the same as depression. Sloth is something long-lasting that causes us to view the good things God gives us – work, relationships, prayer, study of the Bible – as burdensome demands to be escaped from. It makes us look at the place where God has called us, and the people he's called us to be with, with a restless and discontented eye and seek to find a way to wriggle out of what we see as the constraints of our situation. We can do so either by withdrawing, or by burying ourselves in over-activity and finding other ways to fill our time.

Suddenly sloth seems very relevant to life in the West in the 21st century. Which of us hasn't used, for example, scrolling through social media as a 'way to unwind for five minutes' which becomes two hours of our lives we'll never get back, and prevents us from doing the thing we're actually supposed to be doing?

It's not hard to think of other examples of modern manifestations of this ancient vice: the single person's feeling that all would be well if only he or she were married, or the married person's feeling that marital faithfulness is a destructive straightjacket and all would be well if he or she were in a relationship with someone else; the feeling that we would be so much happier if we just found a different job; the all-too-pervasive listlessness experienced in prayer.

Make no mistake. Sloth, with its restless combination of anger and wrong desire is indeed deadly. It's destructive of relationships. It's destructive of work. And it's especially destructive of prayer.

Whilst it's by no means the primary interpretation of the passage from Romans 7, the words still seem to me to describe well someone in the grip of sloth: 'For what I want to do I do not do, but what I hate I do... For I have the desire to do what is good, but I cannot carry it out.' There's that sense of being pulled away, not having the strength to do the thing we know God wants us to do, perhaps deep down not even having the will to try.

Wrestling free

So how can we be free of it? There are some helpful means of grace for us to practise. Praying short, direct prayers so our attention doesn't wander. Setting ourselves short tasks and not stopping until they're complete. Praying that we will again see the work and relationships we have as a source of delight rather than discontent.

Above all, however, as for Paul in his anguished writing, the way we are to be free is by Jesus giving us freedom: 'Thanks be to God through Jesus Christ our Lord.' He alone frees us from the shackles of sloth, brings piercing light to show the way through the fog, and stills our restless hearts to find their rest in him.

QUESTIONS FOR REFLECTION

1. What aspects of sloth can you identify in your own habits?
2. What passages of Scripture could you memorise to help you focus when tempted by sloth?
3. How will remembering the love and grace of God in Christ help you overcome sloth?

PRAYER

Almighty and everlasting God,
you give us grace to know you,
work through which to serve you,
and neighbours to care for:
deliver us from the sin of sloth
and give us instead perseverance to run with joy
the race you set before us,
loving you with our whole heart, mind, soul, and
strength,
that we may bring glory to you in all that we do,
through our Saviour Jesus Christ,
Amen.

Fiona Gibson is vicar of the parishes of Cople, Moggerhanger, and Willington, Archdeacon-designate of Ludlow, and Vice-Chair of the Junia Network.

Jesus's
WORDS
FROM
THE
CROSS

26. Father, Forgive Them

Bible Reading
Matthew 6:9-15

This, then, is how you should pray:
  'Our Father in heaven,
  hallowed be your name,
  your kingdom come,
  your will be done,
      on earth as it is in heaven.
  Give us today our daily bread.
  And forgive us our debts,
      as we also have forgiven our debtors.
  And lead us not into temptation,
      but deliver us from the evil one.'
For if you forgive other people when they sin against you, your heavenly Father will also forgive you. But if you do not forgive others their sins, your Father will not forgive your sins.

Starter Question
Are there limits to forgiveness?

Today's Text
But to you who are listening I say: Love your enemies,
do good to those who hate you, bless those who curse
you, pray for those who mistreat you.
Luke 6:27-28

Two other men, both criminals, were also led out with
him to be executed. When they came to the place called
the Skull, they crucified him there, along with the criminals—one on his right, the other on his left. Jesus said,
'Father, forgive them, for they do not know what they are
doing.' And they divided up his clothes by casting lots.
Luke 23:32-34

Bishop J C Ryle comments: 'It is worthy of remark that as
soon as the blood of the Great Sacrifice began to flow, the
Great High Priest began to intercede.'
We are indeed on holy ground and can only approach medita-
tion on the cross of Jesus in silence, humility, and profound grati-
tude. For here is the heart of our salvation, the source of our forgiveness and our new life. So, before looking at the words of Jesus,
it is only right to pause again and worship.

The blood of Christ
The blood flowing from Jesus's body was his life which he freely
gave up for all humanity; and of course, more personally, for you
and for me. We come as we are to the cross, in all our frailty, with
all our imperfections and our pathetic attempts at living the new
life in Christ. And we confess, we repent, we receive from our dying Saviour. Every sin I have ever committed, the sin that always
separates me from the living God, every sin is forgiven because
Jesus hung on the cross. I am forgiven; I am free; I am clean. Let
us receive again that amazing grace.

Now, let us see Jesus who has just reached the place called the

Skull, exhausted, already in agony from the flogging (scourging). Luke is understated in his account: 'they crucified him there, along with the criminals.' His readers knew exactly what crucifixion entailed: the unspeakable agony of nails roughly hammered through his wrists and ankles and the elevation of the cross which tore at his body. This was excruciating pain and his blood was flowing freely. This was the time he thought about others.

THE FATHER'S FORGIVENESS

This is the only time in the Gospels where Jesus speaks about forgiveness with regard to some people committing an offence against him directly. All through his ministry he shocked the onlookers by pronouncing someone's sins as being forgiven: Luke 5:20, to the paralytic let down by his friends from the roof, 'Friend, your sins are forgiven'; Luke 7:48, to the woman washing his feet with her tears, 'Your sins are forgiven.' And he taught his disciples to forgive: Luke 17:3,4 'If your brother or sister sins against you, rebuke them; and if they repent, forgive them. Even if they sin against you seven times in a day and seven times come back to you saying "I repent", you must forgive them.'

But let us return to Jesus on the cross. He is praying to his father. He is thinking about others and not only consumed by his own agony. He is praying for the soldiers certainly, but probably also, verse 13, 'the chief priests, the rulers and the people.' Jesus prays that God will forgive them. He was certainly obeying his own instruction in Luke 6:28, to 'pray for those who mistreat (abuse) you', and leaving us an example that we might follow in his steps (1 Peter 2:21).

Jesus's first word from the cross takes us straight to a central theme of our faith, forgiveness and reconciliation. We can all rejoice that we are the beneficiaries of his sacrificial death; we can all pray for those who do us wrong, however wounded we have been by them; and we can ask God for the grace to forgive and set free those who sin against us. There's a wideness in God's mercy.

QUESTIONS FOR REFLECTION

1. Have I reached the point where I truly know that all my sins have been forgiven by Jesus on the cross?
2. Am I able to pray for those who have most wounded me in my life and believe that the Father can forgive them?
3. Can I forgive up to seventy seven times?

PRAYER
Almighty Father,
whose son Jesus in the middle of his
horrendous suffering on the cross
was able to pray for his abusers:
strengthen and work in everyone who today struggles
with issues of pain and resentment,
and allow them through the power
flowing from the cross
to cry out to you and trust in you for your healing,
through the same Jesus Christ our Lord
who is now alive and reigns with
you and the Holy Spirit,
one God, now and for ever,
Amen.

Henry Scriven *is General Secretary of EFAC (The Evangelical Fellowship in the Anglican Communion) and Hon. Asst. Bishop in the dioceses of Oxford and Winchester*

27. WITH JESUS IN PARADISE

BIBLE READINGS
Psalm 24:3-5 and Isaiah 1:18

Who may ascend the mountain of the LORD?
Who may stand in his holy place?
The one who has clean hands and a pure heart,
who does not trust in an idol
or swear by a false god.
They will receive blessing from the LORD
and vindication from God their Saviour.

.....

'Come now, let us settle the matter,'
says the LORD.
'Though your sins are like scarlet,
they shall be as white as snow;
though they are red as crimson,
they shall be like wool.'

STARTER QUESTION
Who on earth could belong in paradise?

Today's Text

One of the criminals who hung there hurled insults at him: 'Aren't you the Messiah? Save yourself and us!' But the other criminal rebuked him. 'Don't you fear God,' he said, 'since you are under the same sentence? We are punished justly, for we are getting what our deeds deserve. But this man has done nothing wrong.' Then he said, 'Jesus, remember me when you come into your kingdom.' Jesus answered him, 'Truly I tell you, today you will be with me in paradise.'   *Luke 23:39-43*

He was now so sick that the Governor had approved the removal of his handcuffs. No longer were two Prison Officers required. One was enough, and he could wait outside the hospice room, allowing him to die with dignity. As the cancer had got its grip the prisoner had moved from his cell in HMP Brixton, to a hospital ward and now to a room in a hospice. It was the middle of the night and I sat on the edge of his bed as we looked out on the falling snow. The streetlamps lit the flakes as they fell and settled on the branches of nearby trees. 'I'm scared', he said. He'd long turned his back on the Christian faith of his upbringing. 'Did you know that God could look on your life and see you as pure as that snow?' I asked. He wanted to know how that could be possible. I explained. Later, I asked if he would like to pray the Lord's Prayer with me. He said he would. Never have I heard, 'Forgive us our trespasses', cried out with such urgency.

The criminal on the neighbouring cross recognised how that could be possible on the first Good Friday. Despite his personal agony, he was aware that the man in the middle was the focus of the crowd's attention. The local bigwigs had shown up to scoff. The military had their fun. Nailing him hadn't been enough. Even the other criminal joined in the mockery. He had just enough time left to hurl some abuse and grab a final headline.

RECOGNISING JESUS

In the midst of this mêlée, the scales fell from our criminal's eyes. He recognised the innocence of Jesus. But more than that: he recognised not only his purity but his divinity. And his own guilt and just judgment. When Jesus appeared at his most humiliated and weak, our criminal recognises the scope of his majesty and power. 'Jesus, remember me when you come into your kingdom.'

You may scoff at the scope of Jesus's grace. The first person to trust in the crucified Lord Jesus is a criminal. Really?! If that sticks in your throat, you need to be reminded that throughout Luke's Gospel it is the lost, and life's losers, who are drawn to Jesus. He welcomes them. He transforms them. That is his mission. 'It is not the healthy who need a doctor, but the sick. I have not come to call the righteous, but sinners to repentance' (Luke 5:31-31). It is only the self-satisfied who meet Jesus and miss out.

BEYOND REACH?

Are there some in society you consider to be beyond the reach of Jesus's love and grace? If so, you have lost sight of the magnificence of Jesus. You have also lost sight of your own spiritual bankruptcy. You may have once cried out for grace, with our criminal, to the crucified Jesus. Maybe your inner Pharisee now tries to blend your better bits with his grace as you hope for paradise. You began on your knees. You have developed a strut. In reality you echo only half of the criminal's affirmation. You delight in Jesus's purity— but are rather pleased with your own too.

Or, less perilously but more painfully, your Christian walk lacks confident joy because your awareness of your less lovable bits leads you to question your place in paradise. Progress in holiness is slow and you fear, if not outright condemnation, at best begrudging acceptance. Reflect afresh on the magnificence of Jesus. Remember his mission. He came for the lost, he came for life's losers. The door to paradise is marked 'Sinners Only.' By his grace you belong there.

If your trust is in him you have been washed whiter than snow. Delight in his grace. Grow in his grace. Know that you have a place in paradise. You too have cried out 'Forgive us our trespasses.' He has hidden his face from your sins, and has blotted out all (not a few, not some, but all) your iniquities. Live in the light of your assured place in paradise.

QUESTIONS FOR REFLECTION

1. Is there a type of person you would be horrified to meet in paradise? If so, where is the deficiency in your theology?
2. What stops you delighting in your place in paradise?
3. What would it look like to live in the light of your assured place in paradise?

PRAYER
God our Father,
in your loving kindness you sent your Son
to open the door to paradise:
help us to grasp the breadth of your grace,
that our attitude to others and ourselves
would be transformed,
and that we would live in the light of
our place in paradise,
through the magnificence of our Lord Jesus Christ
who loves and reigns with you,
in the power of the Holy Spirit,
One God, now and always,
Amen.

Phil Chadder *served for many years as Senior Chaplain at HMP Brixton and is now responsible for training Prison Chaplains for the UK Ministry of Justice.*

28. Behold Your Son

Bible Reading
Philippians 2:3-5

Do nothing out of selfish ambition or vain conceit. Rather, in humility value others above yourselves, not looking to your own interests but each of you to the interests of the others. In your relationships with one another, have the same mindset as Christ Jesus:

Who, being in very nature God,

did not consider equality with God something to be used to his own advantage;

rather, he made himself nothing

by taking the very nature of a servant,

being made in human likeness.

And being found in appearance as a man,

he humbled himself

by becoming obedient to death—

even death on a cross!

Therefore God exalted him to the highest place

and gave him the name that is above every name,

that at the name of Jesus every knee should bow,

in heaven and on earth and under the earth,

and every tongue acknowledge that Jesus Christ is Lord,

to the glory of God the Father.

Starter Question
How can we have the mindset of Jesus towards members of our family?

TODAY'S TEXT

When Jesus saw his mother there, and the disciple whom he loved standing nearby, he said to her, "Woman, here is your son," and to the disciple, "Here is your mother." From that time on, this disciple took her into his home.

John 19:26-27

Our text finds us with Jesus on the cross. He has been arrested, found guilty of blasphemy, crucified, and is now dying. Jesus looks at his mother, Mary, and says, 'Woman, behold your son.' At first glance, the reader might think Jesus is referring to himself. After all, he is in a pitiful state—nails in his hands and feet, bloodied from his beatings and scourging, and the end is coming soon. However, Jesus is not referring to himself, rather to his faithful follower, John (the writer of this Gospel). He is indicating to his mother that she is now to regard John as her son and look to him for the obligations of a son.

THINKING OF OTHERS

After speaking to his mother, Jesus looks to John ('the disciple whom Jesus loved' is how John referred to himself) and says: 'Behold, your mother.' Jesus is transferring his earthly responsibility for his mother's well-being to his faithful disciple. Even as he is dying, Jesus is making sure that his human mother is taken care of. As the first-born son, he was responsible to make sure his mother (since his adopted father had died) is provided for and cared for in her old age. The One who came from above and who said he was returning to his Father is making sure his earthly mother is in good hands.

Isn't it amazing that even in his death Jesus was thinking about those he was leaving behind? 'I will not leave you as orphans', he said to his disciples (John 14:18), and now he is saying to his mother that she will not be left alone either. Jesus leaves for his disciples an important example that is often overlooked by his modern day followers. Are we responsible enough to make sure our earthly families are provided for and cared for when we die? Do we take the time to make sure we have a *Last Will and Testament* with instructions on what to do when we are taken home to heaven? This is an important responsibility not just for people who are older in years, but young people as well since we never know when our time to depart planet earth will be.

FINAL TESTIMONY

Our *Last Will and Testament* should give instructions on who should care for one's children (godparents, family members, etc.), how to distribute your assets and possessions, and not least, your testament (witness) of your conversion to Jesus Christ and your walk with him. This is such an important gift to give your children and grandchildren—even in your death for them to hear in your own words how you came to follow Jesus and how you lived for him! Sadly, too many followers of Jesus do not want to think about death, especially their own, and when the unthinkable happens, their families are left not only in grief, but in confusion and helplessness.

Jesus reminds us that, even in his death, he was thinking not of himself, but his precious mother in her grief and old age. Because of this transferring of responsibility, Mary would have a family with whom she could live, and would not have to live in poverty as a beggar.

QUESTIONS FOR REFLECTION
1. What does this passage tell us about Jesus?
2. Why do you think Jesus did not give this responsibility to his brothers (Matthew 12:46)?
3. Do you have a Last Will and Testament of your own?

PRAYER

Look with mercy, O God our Father,
on all whose increasing years bring them weakness,
distress, or isolation
(especially _____).
Provide for *them* homes of dignity and peace;
give *them* understanding helpers,
and the willingness to accept help,
and as *their* strength diminishes,
increase *their* faith and *their* assurance of your love,
through Jesus Christ our Lord,
Amen. [1]

Foley Beach *is the Primate and Archbishop of the Anglican Church in North America (ACNA), and Chair of GAFCON's Primates' Council.*

1   From the ACNA Book of Common Prayer (2019), page 663.

29. The Forsaken Son

Bible Reading
Psalm 22:1-8

For the director of music. To the tune of "The Doe of the Morning."
A psalm of David.

My God, my God, why have you forsaken me?
>   Why are you so far from saving me,
>   so far from my cries of anguish?
My God, I cry out by day, but you do not answer,
>   by night, but I find no rest.
Yet you are enthroned as the Holy One;
>   you are the one Israel praises.
In you our ancestors put their trust;
>   they trusted and you delivered them.
To you they cried out and were saved;
>   in you they trusted and were not put to shame.
But I am a worm and not a man,
>   scorned by everyone, despised by the people.
All who see me mock me;
>   they hurl insults, shaking their heads.
"He trusts in the LORD," they say,
>   "let the LORD rescue him.
Let him deliver him,
>   since he delights in him."

Starter Question
What was the greatest agony that Jesus endured for us?

Today's Text

Two rebels were crucified with him, one on his right and one on his left. Those who passed by hurled insults at him, shaking their heads and saying, 'You who are going to destroy the temple and build it in three days, save yourself! Come down from the cross, if you are the Son of God!' In the same way the chief priests, the teachers of the law and the elders mocked him. 'He saved others,' they said, 'but he can't save himself! He's the king of Israel! Let him come down now from the cross, and we will believe in him. He trusts in God. Let God rescue him now if he wants him, for he said, "'I am the Son of God."' In the same way the rebels who were crucified with him also heaped insults on him.

From noon until three in the afternoon darkness came over all the land. About three in the afternoon Jesus cried out in a loud voice, 'Eli, Eli, lema sabachthani?' (which means 'My God, my God, why have you forsaken me?'). *Matthew 27:38-46*

Ingmar Bergman's 1963 movie, *Winter Light*, is the unrelentingly bleak story of a pastor ministering to a small rural congregation, whilst undergoing an existential crisis. Full of Swedish gloom, and regarded as dreary, turgid, and meandering by critics, *Winter Light* is one of my favourite films. Towards the end, there's a conversation between Tomas, the pastor, and Algot, his handicapped sexton, who's puzzled by Christ's Passion.

'Wouldn't you agree', says Algot, 'that the focus on his suffering is all wrong? This emphasis on physical pain. It may sound presumptuous of me, but in my own humble way, I think I've suffered as much physical pain as Jesus. I feel he was tormented far worse on a different level. Christ's disciples had run away, they'd all abandoned him. He was left all alone. And when Jesus was nailed to the cross, and hung there in torment, he cried out, 'My God, my God, why have you forsaken me?' He thought that his heavenly Father had abandoned him. Surely that must have been the greatest hardship of all? God's silence.'

THE CRY OF DESOLATION
Our familiarity with the Gospel stories of Jesus's death can blunt the shock of his words from the cross. And never more so than in that cry of utter desolation, 'My God, my God, why have you forsaken me?' It comes, in Matthew's narrative, as a kind of culmination of agony—amid the mockery of the chief priests, the teachers of the law, and the elders, amid the insults hurled at Jesus by those crucified with him. It comes, too, amid a darkness that covers all the land. Matthew, like Mark, records Jesus's words in their original Aramaic, and then translates them for his readers—for those eyewitnesses present at the crucifixion, this moment must have seared itself onto their memories.

And how could it not? For the cross of Jesus Christ unsettles all our expectations and neat certainties. Here God crucifies human wisdom, the intellectual arrogance that seeks to dictate to God how he should act in our world. Here God chooses the weak things of the world to shame the strong. God has sent his Son to proclaim the 'good news' and what a curious kind of 'good news' it is. We behold our God, and he is dying on a cross. The promised king reigns from a throne of wood and nails, and the glory of the eternal Son shines in dazzling darkness. In the crucified Christ, God's victory is revealed in defeat, his presence in absence, his power in weakness, his love in wrath, his blessings through curse, his life through death.

THE PAIN OF HELL
What is Jesus enduring, as he speaks these words of dereliction? He is enduring hell. Forget the medieval paintings—those kitsch subterranean lairs awash with red, full of pitchforks and spit roasts. If you want to know what hell looks like, look at Jesus on

the cross. The sky is black, because God is present in judgment. His just wrath is being poured out, the full price for sin is being paid, the full punishment for sin is being borne. And that price is being paid, that punishment is being borne, not by us, but by God himself, in his own flesh. Jesus is not some random man, the unwilling plaything of an abusive Father; but nor does the crucifixion involve some sort of rupture in the life of the eternal Trinity. Rather, on the cross, the truly divine Son is forsaken as true man.

Algot was right—Jesus didn't cry out because of the physical suffering, horrific though it was—the torn flesh, and the loss of blood, and the gradual, agonising process of suffocation. Jesus cried out because he was undergoing something far worse—the unimaginable horror of separation from God, of God turning from him completely. On the cross, Jesus experienced hell for us—he took our place, he died our death, he was abandoned so that we might never be. That's why, as Jesus dies, Matthew records that the curtain of the temple was torn in two, from top to bottom. Because of Jesus's sin-bearing death, the barrier which separated a holy God from sinful man has been broken down once-and-for-all. In Christ, true forgiveness can now be known, and a new life with God can be begun.

The abandonment of the cross is no surprise to Jesus, no unexpected accident of history. Jesus speaks of prophecy fulfilled. His words are those of the Psalmist, from the opening verse of Psalm 22: 'My God, my God, why have you forsaken me?' The cry of desolation is nonetheless still a cry of faith in God, which recognises, even in the depths of darkness and despair, that 'in you our ancestors put their trust, they trusted and you delivered them' (Psalm 22:4). Even here, Jesus teaches us how to pray. When we struggle to know what to say to God, when there appears no consolation in our circumstances or relief amid our afflictions, we can turn to Scripture, and let its words shape ours. And we can pray to the one now risen and exalted, who has been through death and hell for us, whose perfect love casts out our fears.

QUESTIONS FOR REFLECTION

1. How does this passage help you to avoid minimising the seriousness of your sin?
2. How does this passage help you to marvel at the depths of Jesus's love for you?
3. How can you make use of this word from the cross to pray for, or encourage, someone you know who is currently suffering?

PRAYER

Ever-holy and ever-loving God,
you made your Son, who had no sin, to be sin for us,
and to endure forsakenness,
that we might never be forsaken:
mercifully grant to us such confidence in
the cross of our Lord,
that we may know the peace of sins forgiven,
and the joy of life with you forever,
through the same Jesus Christ our Saviour,
Amen.

Mark Smith is the Dean and Director of Studies in Theology at Clare College, Cambridge.

30. The Thirsty Saviour

Bible Reading
Psalm 69:1-4, 13-16

For the director of music. To the tune of "Lilies." Of David.

Save me, O God,
      for the waters have come up to my neck.
I sink in the miry depths, where there is no foothold.
I have come into the deep waters;
      the floods engulf me.
I am worn out calling for help; my throat is parched.
My eyes fail, looking for my God.
Those who hate me without reason
      outnumber the hairs of my head;
many are my enemies without cause,
      those who seek to destroy me.

...

But I pray to you, Lord, in the time of your favour;
in your great love, O God,
      answer me with your sure salvation.
Rescue me from the mire, do not let me sink;
deliver me from those who hate me,
      from the deep waters.
Do not let the floodwaters engulf me
      or the depths swallow me up
      or the pit close its mouth over me.
Answer me, LORD, out of the goodness of your love;
      in your great mercy turn to me.

Starter Question
*What is the motor that kept King David hopeful in the
midst of the scorn of his own people?*

Today's Text

Later, knowing that everything had now been finished,
and so that Scripture would be fulfilled, Jesus said, 'I am
thirsty.' A jar of wine vinegar was there, so they soaked
a sponge in it, put the sponge on a stalk of the hyssop plant, and lifted it to Jesus' lips. When he had received the drink, Jesus said, 'It is finished.' With that, he
bowed his head and gave up his spirit.   *John 19:28-30*

There are different sorts of rejections. There is the kind of
rejection one feels when an enemy blatantly offends you.
We are getting used to the rejection we experience when
we 'interact' through social networks with those who hold different positions about God, life, politics, or even football clubs.
What kind of rejection did Jesus experience at the cross when he
said that he was thirsty? The apostle John tells us that the words
'I thirst' were said in order to fulfil the Scriptures. But what were
they fulfilling? What was going on in Psalm 69 in a shadow form
which reached its complete meaning when Jesus experienced that
desperate dryness of the tongue and mouth while dying?

Jesus and the Psalm

Psalm 69:8-9 tells us that the reason why King David was despised
was because of his zeal for seeing the restoration of the adoration
in Jerusalem:

I am a foreigner to my own family,
a stranger to my own mother's children;
for zeal for your house consumes me,
and the insults of those who insult you fall on me.

But Psalm 69:20-21 not only tells us why David was being scorned,
but also how he was suffering. The suffering was coming from
those within his life. His brothers, his own people were treating
him as an alien and that made the suffering even worse:

Scorn has broken my heart
    and has left me helpless;
I looked for sympathy, but there was none,
    for comforters, but I found none.
They put gall in my food
    and gave me vinegar for my thirst.

As a King, David was the incarnation of God's plans for Israel and the world. Thus in a very real way, the dissatisfaction people had with God fell on David's shoulders.

JESUS AND US

The apostle John is connecting the dots. Jesus, the Son of David, also suffered the consequences of his people's lack of desire for God and his kingdom. Their lack of zeal took someone greater than David to an even greater suffering: the cross. The rebellion of humans against God, that was partially experienced by David, reached its climactic moment when verbalised by the lips of our thirsty crucified Saviour. This is why John says Scriptures were fulfilled.

Dear brothers and sisters, in order to have the blessed life Jesus offers, we have to acknowledge that our rebellious hearts have the tendency to desire an average and lukewarm sort of spirituality over his exuberant and reverberating life. 'On the last and greatest day of the festival, Jesus stood and said in a loud voice, "Let anyone who is thirsty come to me and drink"' (John 7:37). The rest of the Gospel of John reaffirms what John said at the beginning: 'He came to that which was his own, but his own did not receive him' (1:11).

In the face of our rejection of him, Jesus went one step further. The Servant King would come to assume our sinfulness upon himself as a perfect substitute for our sins. As our substitute, he suffered what we should suffer in order to restore the adoration of God, by his people in his Father's house. At the cross, our Lord experienced the consequences that we justly deserve for our lack of zeal for God's Kingdom: eternal thirst. He took on himself the epitome of the dissatisfaction that our ungrateful passion for God deserves so that we may get the eternal satisfaction as children of God.

Is it not amazing that our Lord was willing to suffer all that in order to show us what real zeal for God and his kingdom looks like? Dear friend, at the cross, Jesus drank the sour wine in order that the promise of us tasting a new one in his presence forever may be certain and true. Therefore let us come to him as the well from which flows streams of living water in order that our half-hearted desires for the establishment of his Father's Kingdom may be renewed and revived, for his glory and the sake of the nations.

Questions for Reflection

1. What are the main reasons why you don't hunger and thirst more for God and his kingdom?
2. What are the symptoms of a Christian that is not satisfied with God and his kingdom?
3. How does Jesus's persistent love for making you part of his kingdom encourage and challenge you?

PRAYER
Glorious and All-Sufficient Father,
who out of the happiness you had from eternity
in the fellowship of the Son and the Holy Spirit
sent Jesus to offer us salvation and everlasting life:
grant in us the awareness of our lukewarm affection
towards you and your kingdom,
so that motivated by your gospel
into repentance and faith
you may lead us into a constant progress in our desire
for following your Son despite the costs,
for your glory, our satisfaction in you, and the sake of
the nations,
in Jesus name,
Amen.

Cristóbal Cerón Pi is minister of Iglesia Santiago Apóstol and Rector of the Centro de Estudios Pastorales (Centre for Pastoral Studies) in the Iglesia Anglicana de Chile.

31. It Is Finished

Bible Reading
John 19:28-37

Later, knowing that everything had now been finished, and so that Scripture would be fulfilled, Jesus said, 'I am thirsty.' A jar of wine vinegar was there, so they soaked a sponge in it, put the sponge on a stalk of the hyssop plant, and lifted it to Jesus' lips. When he had received the drink, Jesus said, 'It is finished.' With that, he bowed his head and gave up his spirit.

Now it was the day of Preparation, and the next day was to be a special Sabbath. Because the Jewish leaders did not want the bodies left on the crosses during the Sabbath, they asked Pilate to have the legs broken and the bodies taken down. The soldiers therefore came and broke the legs of the first man who had been crucified with Jesus, and then those of the other. But when they came to Jesus and found that he was already dead, they did not break his legs. Instead, one of the soldiers pierced Jesus' side with a spear, bringing a sudden flow of blood and water. The man who saw it has given testimony, and his testimony is true. He knows that he tells the truth, and he testifies so that you also may believe. These things happened so that the scripture would be fulfilled: 'Not one of his bones will be broken,' and, as another scripture says, 'They will look on the one they have pierced.'

Starter Question
What has Jesus finished?

Today's Text

Jesus said, 'It is finished.' With that, he bowed his head and gave up his spirit.   *John 19:30*

'I t is finished.' This phrase was the conquering cry of our Lord Jesus Christ as he died on the cross for all who would ever believe in him. These three words remind us that there is nothing we can do to earn our salvation. Our Lord and Saviour Jesus Christ has done everything that he needed to do for our redemption.

The finished work of salvation

John writes that before the Roman 'colonial' soldiers arrested Jesus, he prayed his last public prayer to the Father saying 'I have brought you glory on earth by finishing the work you gave me to do' (John 17:4). Jesus specifically asks the Father to glorify him (recognise him) for finishing the work that God had given him to do on earth. This event was a 'triumphant climax' that merited a special 'milestone.'

Doctor Luke and the Apostle Paul remind us that the work Jesus (the Son of Man) had been sent to do was 'to seek and to save the lost' (Luke 19:10), to be 'a sacrifice of atonement, through the shedding of his blood—to be received by faith' (Romans 3:25), and to reconcile sinful people to a Holy God. The Apostle Paul adds when writing to the Corinthians: 'All this is from God, who reconciled us to himself through Christ and gave us the ministry of reconciliation: that God was reconciling the world to himself in Christ, not counting people's sins against them. And he has committed to us the message of reconciliation' (2 Corinthians 5:18-19). Only God in the flesh could undertake and complete such a unique role.

Further completed was the fulfilment of all Old Testament prophecies and predictions of the coming liberator (Messiah). Beginning from the book of Genesis to Malachi, over three hundred detailed prophecies predicting the coming of Jesus are fulfilled. From the 'offspring' who would 'crush the serpent's head' (Genesis 3:15), to the suffering servant in Isaiah, to the prediction of John the Baptist, the 'messenger' of the Lord who would 'prepare the way' for the messiah—all are fulfilled and finished at the cross.

THE COMPLETED VICTORY

Although the redemption of humankind is the most crucial finished undertaking, many other things were completed at the cross. The sufferings Jesus endured and especially in his last hours, were finished. God's will for Jesus was finished in his perfect obedience to the Father. Jesus himself alludes to his 'obedience' to the Father when he says 'for I seek not to please myself but him who sent me' (John 5:30). Then again, he adds, 'I have come down from heaven not to do my will but to do the will of him who sent me' (John 6:38).

Most importantly, Satan and the power of sin was finished. No longer would humankind have to feel the pain of the 'flaming arrows of the evil one' (Ephesians 6:16). This agony is now totally extinguished by the shield of faith in Jesus, who has finished everything. By holding up the 'shield of faith' in the Jesus who finished the work of redemption, we can, by faith, live as new creations in Christ. Jesus Christ's finished work on the cross was the beginning of new life for all who were once 'dead in your transgressions and sins' but who are now 'made alive with Christ' (Ephesians 2:1, 5). Moreover, lest we forget 'it is by grace, you have been saved' (Ephesians 2:8).

Whatever needs to be done has been done by Christ. The debt is paid; forgiveness is offered to all. Nothing remains for us to do but to put our trust in the finished work of the cross which God has accepted. It is finished. No 'if' or 'but' or 'maybe'—victory over sin and death has been won for us. Therefore, it is finished indeed.

QUESTIONS FOR REFLECTION

1. How did the achievement of the cross upset the expectations of Jesus's enemies?
2. Why could his death not be the end of the story?
3. What impact does it have on our Christian lives when we forget his finished work for us?

PRAYER

Almighty God, redeemer of humankind,
whose Son Jesus Christ finished the work for our
salvation on the cross,
paying the full price for our sins,
and offering us the gift of eternal life:
grant that we, who proclaim his
death for our salvation,
may also heed his call to take up
our cross and follow him;
through Jesus Christ, our Lord,
Amen.

Timothy Wambunya is the Vicar of St Paul with Christ Church, Slough and former Bishop of Butere in Western Kenya. He is the founder and chair of trustees of the African Institute for Contemporary Mission and Research (AICMAR) and editor of The Big Issues Impacting the Growth of the Church.

32. In The Father's Hands

Bible Reading

1 Corinthians 1:18-25

For the message of the cross is foolishness to those who are perishing, but to us who are being saved it is the power of God. For it is written:

"I will destroy the wisdom of the wise;

the intelligence of the intelligent I will frustrate."

Where is the wise person? Where is the teacher of the law? Where is the philosopher of this age? Has not God made foolish the wisdom of the world? For since in the wisdom of God the world through its wisdom did not know him, God was pleased through the foolishness of what was preached to save those who believe. Jews demand signs and Greeks look for wisdom, but we preach Christ crucified: a stumbling block to Jews and foolishness to Gentiles, but to those whom God has called, both Jews and Greeks, Christ the power of God and the wisdom of God. For the foolishness of God is wiser than human wisdom, and the weakness of God is stronger than human strength.

Starter Question

Jews demand signs and Greeks look for wisdom, but what does your society or subculture look for?

Today's Text

It was now about noon, and darkness came over the whole land until three in the afternoon, for the sun stopped shining. And the curtain of the temple was torn in two. Jesus called out with a loud voice, 'Father, into your hands I commit my spirit.' When he had said this, he breathed his last.   *Luke 23:44-46*

When you think of God, what do you picture? We all want beauty; something so bright we fall to our knees before it. Something bigger than us; the kind that makes us shield our eyes but look and look and look again. We never grow out of this yearning; but it takes different forms. The newborn reaches for her mother's earring. The toddler is transfixed by Christmas lights. Teens scroll furiously through pages of Insta-perfection.

The Bible says we're made to worship and it's beauty that captures our hearts. But be careful what you gaze upon: Those who worship idols become like them (Psalm 115:8). Worship strength and you'll have no truck with weakness. Worship physical beauty and you'll spend everything on your appearance. Worship relationships and you'll be destroyed when others let you down.

The question is always 'Who is God?' And it's a question you must answer whether you subscribe to 'a religious outlook' or not. But how should we answer? The Bible gives a surprising route to knowing God: the cross!

Knowing God at the cross

We naturally look for power and wisdom, and a particularly human kind of power and wisdom. But as Paul wrote in 1 Corinthians 1, God reveals himself at the cross as a God who subverts all our expectations. We thought he'd press down on the world with strength, instead he shows up in solidarity with the downtrodden. We thought he'd raise himself up with wisdom, instead he is content to be considered a curse and a by-word.

Want to know God? Look to the cross—that is the Christian approach. And with today's word from the cross we are led into the deepest truths about God. The heart of it all is Christ, the obedient Son, praying "Father."

Here is Christ doing what sons are meant to do: he is reverently submitting. Having accomplished all that the Father has given him to do he is acknowledging that everything has come from on high and everything must be returned back. "For from him and through him and for him are all things. To him be the glory forever! Amen" (Romans 11:36).

This is the Son's heartbeat. As he entered the world he said 'Here I am—it is written about me in the scroll—I have come to do your will, my God' (Hebrews 10:7). And he carried that attitude all the way to the cross. As he entrusted his life to the Father, so he entrusts his death. In this prayer we have a window onto God's life. At the cross we see into the deepest realities of life: the Son entrusting his spirit to the Father. As Hebrews 9:14 describes it, 'Christ... through the eternal Spirit, offered himself unblemished to God.'

So then, as Jesus prays 'Father', so we are invited in. In fact, the whole point of the cross is that we, through this sacrifice, may join Jesus in his relationship with the Father. Just as he prays 'My Father', now we pray 'Our Father', because we pray in his name.

APPROACHING GOD

How will I approach God? In my own name and according to my own obedience and worth? That is spiritual death. If I'm a legalist, I'll imagine a God all about rules and I'll live and die by my performance. If I'm insecure, I'll imagine an arms-length God, always holding back and I'll be desperate for approval. If I trust my feelings, I'll imagine a God who might deliver on emotional fulfilment, but only if I can work up enough faith or feelings of my own.

The unconditional love of an earthly father gives us a wonderful start. But the unconditional love of a heavenly Abba changes everything. To a distant Power I might bow my head in fear. But the love of my Father makes me fall, rejoicing, to my knees.

QUESTIONS FOR REFLECTION
1. What false pictures of God are you most tempted towards?
2. What picture of God does the cross of Jesus reveal?
3. How does the unconditional love of our Abba change how we think and live day to day?

PRAYER
Our God and heavenly Father,
whose Son, Jesus Christ, gave himself in love
upon the cross:
fill us with his Spirit
that we too may know your fatherly goodness
and yield our own lives in joyful service to the world,
through Jesus Christ our Lord,
Amen.

Emma Scrivener is the author of several books, including A New Name, *and* A New Day *(IVP). She blogs about identity, faith, and mental health at emmascrivener.net.*

FOUNDATIONS OF
FAITH

Reflections on the 39 Articles

A stellar cast of Anglican pastors and theologians from around the world reflect on the foundational teachings of global Anglicanism. Putting the Thirty-nine Articles in their biblical and historical context, they navigate some of the difficult terrain with clear and compelling application for today. This book is an excellent guide for the new-comer, and a refreshing commentary for the seasoned interpreter. With Bible readings, questions for discussion or reflection, and prayers for each chapter.

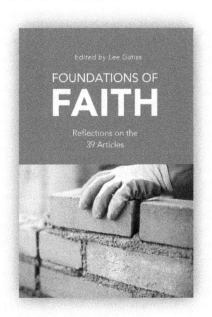

"Foundations of Faith is compulsory reading for all clergy in my diocese in the Church of Nigeria, and there are exams on it for canons and archdeacons. We rejoice greatly in this testimony of our Anglican faith and in the courage of Church Society in a militantly secular Europe."

**Ben Kwashi, General Secretary of GAFCON
and Bishop of Jos.**

Church
Society

EQUIPPING GOD'S
PEOPLE TO LIVE
GOD'S WORD

Church Society

EQUIPPING GOD'S
PEOPLE TO LIVE
GOD'S WORD

offering strategic leadership

For more than 180 years, Church Society has been contending to reform and renew the Church of England in biblical faith, on the basis of its Reformed foundations as expressed in the doctrine of the Articles, the worship of the Prayer Book, and the ministry of the Ordinal.

To find out more and to join Church Society, please visit our website, churchsociety.org

resourcing today's church

Church Society publishes several new books each year, bringing the best of our Anglican Evangelical heritage to new generations, and responding to new pressures and opportunities in today's Church and nation. We also produce a weekly podcast, a quarterly magazine and a theological journal, as well as our regular blog.

serving tomorrow's church

As part of our commitment to raising up a new generation of leaders, we host the annual Junior Anglican Evangelical Conference for those in the early stages of ministry. Church Society also has patronage of around 130 parishes, helping to protect evangelical ministry in the Church of England for the future.

Lightning Source UK Ltd.
Milton Keynes UK
UKHW020642310522
403779UK00010B/742